Am I Teaching Yet?

Stories from the Teacher-Training Trenches

Edited by Molly Hoekstra

HEINEMANN
Portsmouth, NH

Heinemann
A division of Reed Elsevier Inc.
361 Hanover Street
Portsmouth, NH 03801-3912
www.heinemann.com

Offices and agents throughout the world

Library of Congress Cataloging-in-Publication Data
  Am I teaching yet? : stories from the teacher-training trenches / edited by Molly Hoekstra.
    p. cm.
  ISBN 0-325-00402-1 (alk. paper)
    1. Student teaching—United States—Anecdotes.   2. Teachers—Training of—United States—Anecdotes.   I. Hoekstra, Molly, 1970–

LB2157 .U5 A72   2002
370′.71—dc21   2002004348

Editor: Lois Bridges
Production: Vicki Kasabian
Cover design: Jenny Jensen Greenleaf
Typesetter: TechBooks
Manufacturing: Steve Bernier

Printed in the United States of America on acid-free paper
06 05 04 03 02 VP 1 2 3 4 5

Am I Teaching Yet?

Dedicated to

Joanne Fitch, the teacher I would like to be

Doug Hoekstra, my best friend and greatest support

And to all of those in the trenches—learning to help others learn

Contents

....

Acknowledgments   *xi*

Introduction   *xiii*

I. ANTICIPATION

The Student Teacher, Chantelle Edwards   1
Laurie Stapleton

Dissecting the Teaching Experience   4
Jeremy Paschke

Notes to My Master Teachers   8
Shana Ferguson

Olympia's Gift   13
Anne Holzman

Am I Necessary? A Topic of Debate   17
Carla M. Panciera

Poco a Poco   21
Jessica Ferrar

Mission to Mars: An Excerpt from My Student
Teaching Journal   25
Ainslie Cole

II. LIVING LIFE IN THE FAST LANE

Chiffon Bit the Para   27
Barbara Tramonte

Best and Brightest   36
Jorge Verlenden

Contents

Give Me a B   41
Carol Schwalberg

One Step at a Time   48
Anina Robb

The Advantages of Deep Water Swimming   52
Gwynn Gacosta

From the Mouths of Students   59
Mark Sutton

Theme for English 9   64
Carolyn Alessio

Dollars and Points   70
Marcus Goodyear

III. TO TEACH OR NOT TO TEACH

Going to the Library   76
Dee Birch Cameron

Delivering the Truth: Confessions of a Teaching Fellow   81
John Keats

Counter-Inquisitive   87
Sean Whitson

Awakening   91
AP

Why I'm Sorry I Don't Teach English   99
Carol L. Skolnick

To Be or Not to Be a Teacher   103
Jane Goldenberg

IV. REFLECTIONS ON THE BEGINNINGS

The Template in My Head   109
Marcia Worth-Baker

Contents

Michael, the Student Who Pushed Me on as a
Teacher of Reading   113
Alis Headlam

The Ed Block   117
Beverly Carol Lucey

A Classroom Exchange   120
Dennis Donoghue

Street Syllabus   125
Tekla Dennison Miller

We Learn from Our Mistakes   130
Susan C. Voorhees

Thanks to Kay   135
Alexa L. Sandmann

V. FINAL WORD OF ADVICE

Duty Free   140
Davi Walders

Acknowledgments

Although my contribution is slight in comparison to that of the essay writers, I would like to extend my gratitude to a few individuals who directly or indirectly helped this book come to fruition. I would like to thank the faculty and staff and Belmont University, including Dr. Jackie Palka, Dr. Guy Rose, and Dr. Trevor Hutchins, for inspiring my entry into teaching, which in turn led me to editing this book. Thank you to Joanne Fitch, Su Williams, and my students at Walnut Grove Elementary and Buena Vista Paideia School for mentoring me through my own student teaching experience. Thank you to my mother, an exemplary teacher, for her guidance and wisdom. Thanks to Doug Hoekstra, as always, for his unending encouragement. Most important, I would like to thank all the teachers and writers who submitted essays for consideration in this anthology. I wish I had room for every voice! Last, and most graciously, I would like to thank Lois Bridges, my editor at Heinemann. Working with her has been a writer's dream!

Introduction

....

Student teaching can be the worst experience of your career.

These were the words of caution I heard from fellow students and some veteran teachers during the months that led up to my student teaching assignment. As a nontraditional postbaccalaureate student, I was perhaps filled with a more pressing zeal than some of my contemporaries. I was more than eager to enter this world of student teaching and excited to meet the challenges offered. Yet, I worried, *Could their words be true?* Was I about to embark on a terrible journey?

With such a dismal warning, I headed to the bookstore, wanting to find anecdotal evidence to confirm or hopefully deny this generalization. Unfortunately, no books matched my needs. I found a few guides to student teaching, but none showed the real experience behind the tips. I wanted to hear from those who had been through it. Those who had survived. What I wanted to read were the *stories*.

So, I took the words of Toni Morrison to heart: "If there is a book that you want to read and it hasn't been written yet, then you must write it." Or in my case, edit it. Thus, I began to contemplate culling a collection of pieces that would constitute the kind of prose I had hoped to find. I set out to compile a book of truthful glimpses into the world of teacher training.

Fortunately, there exist many writers who teach and teachers who write. And as individuals began to answer my call for manuscripts, I began to collect more than stories. I discovered at my disposal a cadre of teachers, whose experiences and reflections prepared me for my own journey. Indeed, having these manuscripts available to read prior to and during my own student teaching experience was a treasure beyond value. For instance, I knew that no matter how trying my future student teaching placement may be, I was unlikely to have a day as lousy as Tekla Dennison Miller had when she lost her entire class, as described in "Street Syllabus." I found solace in the experience of Susan Voorhees, whose observed lesson ran amuck, but who ultimately became a teacher of student teachers. I hoped to learn from a student like Olympia, in Anne Holzman's "Olympia's Gift."

As I read through manuscripts from people who taught as graduate students or through nontraditional programs designed to meet a teaching shortage, I saw a need to broaden the scope of the anthology to include these voices. Many of my own friends and colleagues were beginning their careers without the luxury of preparation afforded by traditional programs. Essays in Section 2, "Living Life in the Fast Lane," tell the tales of such teachers, as well as the trials and triumphs of new teachers embarking upon learning in the classroom.

Perhaps as some sort of karmic justice for seeking out voices for this book, my own student teaching experience was ideal. For my kindergarten placement, I studied under the most amazing teacher I have ever observed. My fifth-grade mentor was a pillar of support. Thankfully, I can count my student teaching experience among one of the most rewarding times of my life.

As I write this introduction, however, I am in my own first year of teaching, which has had both humbling and harrowing beginnings. The respect that I have for teachers has increased exponentially as I have experienced the profession firsthand. As a writer, I have had many different kinds of employment and I must say that teaching is just about the most difficult, challenging endeavor I have undertaken. Of course, the logical and oft-heard second part of that statement is that teaching is also among the most rewarding of professions. However, I'm not sure I can personally subscribe to this—yet.

In the current political climate, when standardized test scores seem more important than children and where teachers are not trusted to practice their profession, I'm not certain I want to participate in such a system on a long-term basis. The stress of feeling new and often unsure in an intellectually and emotionally complex profession can be overwhelming. Then again, perhaps my strength as a reflective practitioner has merely gone awry as I overanalyze every step I take in the classroom. This job is just so *important.* Essays in Section 3, "To Teach or Not to Teach," probe the question I consider each day: *Where will my path ultimately lead?*

But throughout my educational experience, I have been uncommonly graced with the opportunity to utilize these stories (as well as many others not included in this volume) as a road map. I feel even more fortunate to be able to share them with others who are considering or have embraced teaching as a career. Each story in this collection is unique, yet each reflects the collective experience of those striving to help others learn. I hope you will benefit from and delight in reading these pieces as much as I have.

The Student Teacher, Chantelle Edwards

Laurie Stapleton

Clearly, Chantelle did not expect the big red A circled on the top of her paper, a personal essay about her involvement with the African American Club. African Americans were a minority on campus, and this club had helped promote Black cultural awareness, expand Chantelle's knowledge of her culture's history, and raise her self-esteem. She had written a moving essay, and it was clear she put strong effort into it, deserving of an A. I watched the happiness sweep through her as she quickly read my comments, and her contained grin expanded to a wide smile before she finally turned to show her friends her grade.

Chantelle was adorable. She couldn't have been any taller than 5 feet 1 inch. She was dark-skinned and had pretty, large brown eyes and a smile that would stop you in your tracks. She could be energetic and lively or contemplative and serious. From the corner of my eye I saw Chantelle finally look at me. I knew she was studying me and had decided to trust me because I had recognized not only her efforts in writing, but something significant and meaningful in her life. As a result, Chantelle would begin to trust and believe in herself. She developed a new posture in class and became even more participatory.

Because I was a student teacher, my master teacher had encouraged me to follow her lesson plans, to which I happily agreed. Not only did this save me work, but also her units were full of creative activities. One day during a discussion on the symbolism of color in a poem we were reading, some students regurgitated what they'd learned about white and black as symbolized in *Moby Dick:* white

1

meant purity and all things good, and black meant dark, evil, and all things bad.

Chantelle raised her hand.

"Miss Stapleton, why is black always symbolized as dark and evil in literature?"

The pain behind Chantelle's question tightened my stomach. I squelched it with a trick my master teacher had recently taught me. "Good question. Can anyone offer an answer?"

The class, mostly Hispanic and Caucasian with only two African American girls, was unusually quiet. Not a single hand rose as eyes hid their gaze against the safety of pressboard desks. We were all suddenly acutely aware of the history we wanted to ignore, of the tangible pain in someone we knew and liked, and perhaps of the intangible pain in ourselves.

"No one has any ideas?" I gently repeated, trying to hide my tone of prayer.

Still no response. Fingers twirled nervously, and I attempted to alleviate the tension.

"*Dark, evil,* and *all things bad* are three different concepts. Let's take the concept of darkness. Imagine a closet with no lights on, or a very dark alley. What would you see?"

Still there was silence. I called on a student. "Jeff, what color would you see?"

"I don't know. I guess black." Jeff was agitated, and I realized immediately I shouldn't have singled out a student to help save myself in such an uncomfortable discussion.

"Sure. And symbolically, if a person can't see, he is lost. So in this case, the color black would symbolize being lost."

The students were lost to what I was saying, and so was I for that matter. If the students weren't aware that I was trying to dodge the real question like a politician, they at least knew I didn't usually speak in such an aloof and unclear manner. I resented feeling the need to avoid Chantelle's concern. But she wouldn't let me avoid it.

She said again, "But it just seems like black always symbolizes evil and bad. Why is that?"

As her question drilled into the pit of my stomach, my brain emptied itself of rhetorical answers and my heart filled with the truth she craved and deserved, the truth that would put so many things into perspective for her. I paused, but all I could say to Chantelle was simply, "I don't know." My words seemed to echo loudly in the silent classroom. "It's pretty stupid, isn't it?"

"Yes, it is," she said quietly.

I abandoned my master teacher's agenda then and knew immediately I would follow my heart in all future lessons. I attempted to lead the discussion toward different symbols, not involving color, but the tone for the remaining twelve minutes of the period had been set. Students' participation was minimal, and when at last the bell rang they filed out quietly, in sharp contrast to their jovial exits on every other day of that semester.

The classroom was still. I sat alone at my master teacher's desk. In the clamor of voices outside at lunch I usually heard the voices of students in my class, voices I loved that were eager to talk but today were silenced with a knowledge they may not have articulated, but perhaps more importantly, they *felt*. I realized that I, too, had been silenced by Chantelle's question, and that silence was something to be relied on—consciously or not—to perpetuate the status quo. My title was *student teacher*, but Chantelle had been one of *my* student teachers. I knew I would let my heart, and not my head, guide me in the future.

LAURIE STAPLETON *has taught traditional and alternative high school for eight years. She has published this and five other chapters from her memoir-in-progress,* One Teacher's Journey Through an All-American City, *which depicts her experiences teaching in the San Joaquin Valley and which is also her creative thesis in the M.F.A. program at Goddard College. She currently teaches at California State University Monterey Bay.*

Dissecting the Teaching Experience

Jeremy Paschke

I spent most of my observation hours with Mr. Sullivan, the physics teacher at Roseville Area High School in Roseville, Minnesota. Toward the end of the day, however, I was free to wander through other science classes. On the uppermost shelf in Mr. Journey's biology class I spied a small, innocuous box bearing the label: "Danger. Baby Rattlers."

"Go ahead, have a look," said Mr. Journey. His observant eye had identified the object of my attention. "Just be careful, they bite."

I stood on a chair, then stepped over to the counter. Suddenly, I towered over his class of sophomores, most of whom were occupied with a photosynthesis laboratory. One student caught my eye, noted my proximity to the rattlers, and grinned. Slowly, I leaned forward, peering into the box until its contents became visible. My cheeks blushed. Four plastic rattles sat in the box's bottom, rattles made especially for babies.

Mr. Journey laughed.

"Don't worry," he said, as he walked away to help a student find a chloroplast. "Everyone gets bitten."

The episode in Mr. Journey's class marked the beginning of my seventh week student teaching. I had spent many hours at the back of classrooms, watching the panache that these science teachers effortlessly added to their daily presentations. Mr. Edlund told stories of his welding business when he taught chemical bonds. Mrs. Zummer used a rubber balloon and a student's frizzy hair to bring humor to her discussion of electrical attraction.

Good teachers, I discovered, do not merely give information, they give a part of themselves. Good teachers grab hold of adolescent restlessness and talkative natures, and use them to positive ends. Unfortunately, seven years of postsecondary schooling had inundated me to the university style of teaching, where professors pontificate and pupils pay heed. In a typical college class, no one dares to interrupt the one-way flow of information.

For weeks prior to my student teaching, I planned extensively how I would avoid the lecturing paradigm. But when the moment came, all my planning was for naught, and I retreated into the teaching style that I knew best. I stood at the head of the class and dryly informed my audience how mechanical waves interfere. Students listened, but only as a courtesy. Jenny Kime, a girl who preferred to sit in the back row, gave me an insouciant stare. Her friends fairly oozed out of their seats. My students were wholly indifferent to the scientific principles of superposition.

So it went, week after week, topic after topic, the brilliant teachers around me naturally keeping their classes active and interested, me laboring through lectures.

One Friday afternoon Mr. Sullivan and I shared ideas on how we could introduce the chapter on electricity.

"It's always a tough topic for the kids," said Mr. Sullivan, "because they can't see electricity."

"It was tough for the early scientists too," I said.

Throughout college I had read extensively about the history of physics. Often I shared anecdotes with Mr. Sullivan because he expressed interest in knowing—which was more than I could say for the students.

"It wasn't until Volta's first battery in 1800 when the craze over animal electricity finally died down."

"What's animal electricity?" Mr. Sullivan asked.

"When a dissected frog is set on a metal table and touched with a metal scalpel, the frog's legs convulse," I explained. "The convulsions are caused by a difference in electrical potential, conveyed through the dissimilar metals. Scientists originally thought they were bringing life to a dead creature."

Mr. Sullivan reclined in his chair. He was obviously enjoying every word, so I continued.

"Luigi Galvani discovered the effect in 1790, coining the phrase, *animal electricity*. People were fascinated. Scientists the world over could hardly find enough frogs to dissect. A few years later, Alessandro Volta entered the scene. Volta claimed that the convulsions were created when the metal table connected with the metal scalpel. The frog's nerves and muscles acted as the bridge."

"Neat story," Mr. Sullivan said.

I left school that Friday happy to have shared a story with my colleague. Not until Sunday afternoon did I think of sharing the story with my students.

I was relaxing with a novel when a particular phrase reminded me of my eighth-grade English teacher and her singular rule for quality creative writing: *Show, don't tell*. I knew exactly what I would do in class the next day. I donned my coat, and drove to the store.

On Monday morning, as soon as the bell rang, I strolled to the center of the classroom and asked the students to gather around me. With a 1790s lithograph of Galvani's laboratory projected on the screen overhead, I set the stage for a tale about animal electricity. I told the students that dissecting frogs was cutting-edge science in the eighteenth century, just like genetic engineering is cutting-edge science today. I told them that watching a dead frog convulse was prime entertainment for audiences of all ages.

A murmur circulated the classroom.

"In physics we like to re-create great episodes in science." I reached for a small box that was covered with traces of mud. "Finding frogs in Minnesota is no problem—so many lakes to choose from."

Students uttered their disbelief. Jenny Kime stood up to gain a better view.

"Let me find us a victim. . . ."

I fished around in the box, darting my hand from side to side.

"Slippery little guys." I was grinning from ear to ear, and the whole class waited to see what was coming next. "Ah, I've got one."

Lifting it by its rear from the box, I revealed to the class a green, rubber frog.

"These frogs don't smell so bad," I announced through a chorus of groans. "Let's go ahead with the dissection."

I invited a student to sever the frog's head with scissors. Jenny Kime volunteered to fill the body with lemon juice, an ideal conductor of electricity, to simulate the frog's nerve and muscle tissue.

"Did Galvani stimulate any other animals?" "How can you make the convulsions stronger?" Questions tumbled out into the open. We answered several of the questions through experimentation, like a real scientist would, using our rubber frog, lemon juice, metal nails, and an ammeter with a deflecting needle.

When the time came to write some notes on voltage, not one student complained. They were curious and ready to learn. Professor Galvani might have failed at bringing life to his amphibious subjects; however, in science, failure is a necessary step toward success. By teaching about Galvani's studies and showing my students the genesis of electrical awareness, I certainly succeeded at bringing life to my classroom.

JEREMY PASCHKE *earned a master of science and teaching license from the University of Minnesota. After teaching outside the Twin Cities for one year, he moved to the Chicago area. Currently, Jeremy teaches science at York High School in Elmhurst, Illinois. Jeremy enjoys teaching most when he can surprise his students.*

Notes to My Master Teachers

Shana Ferguson

Dear Mr. ——,

Being in your class is easy. I follow your pace, your rules and standards, your grading, your coattails. I am tougher than I would have been, calmer than I have ever been in a classroom. You are so certain that you are the best that I begin to believe that you are.

Do you remember the other day, during the quiz? That one where maybe Crystal and Candy were cheating? Where maybe Crystal was writing the answers on notebook paper, but I wasn't sure? And then Crystal got up and threw the paper away? In my mind, I was plotting to wait until class was out and then to rummage in the trash, searching for incriminating evidence. But then I forgot. It slipped my mind and I couldn't nab them red-handed to show how smart I was, how omniscient I am at the front of the room, sitting at your desk.

You should be proud of me, though. They turned in identical copies of a worksheet, and I gave them a zero instead of a check or a check plus plus. If I had been you, I would have boomed out to the class "Crystal, put that paper away, or you'll both get zeroes." Where you would have been certain, I am still unsure, wanting to be fair, to avoid open conflict.

Ms. Ferguson

Dear Ms. ——,

When you asked me, or really sort of assigned me, a seven-week unit in your class, I was resentful. Not because I couldn't do it. Of course I can—look how beautifully I do in Mr. ——'s class. But because I thought you wanted a break, an excuse to stay at home an extra hour, to grade papers for your other class. You haven't given much to this class, and then you handed them to me, a dozen slow-moving, feet-dragging, resistant and resentful learners.

And after that first day with them, you told me to be tougher, to be meaner, to send them out if they talked while I talked, if they didn't listen. And that made me even more resentful, because you had never sent them out, but had only threatened and cajoled, wheedled and bribed momentary respite from their antics. I thought I had at least been stronger than you. Why wasn't that enough?

So I've tried to toughen up. By Friday, Luis raised his hand during the quiz and asked, "Did you get up on the wrong side of the bed or something?" My reply was "I am meaner on Fridays." I don't think I'm fooling them, though. I keep them after class sometimes, eat a piece of their lunchtime. I try to talk to them about being quiet, listening, respecting the class. They nod. One boy refuses to say anything, he just raises his thumb as though to say, "Okay, I got ya" in a Fonzi sort of way.

I think my problem is that I want to burst out laughing sometimes. It's so funny, me being mean and them trying to be bad in a gangsta, rap sort of way. I know they are angry about being in ESL, and they know they're stuck, at least for this year.

Ms. Ferguson

Hey, Mr. ——,

Yeah, you. You did it again today, used me like some sort of puppet or poster child.

"Why can't we read *I Know What You Did Last Summer?*" the students whined after you mentioned we had a class set in the library.

"I'll think about it," you said. "Maybe in the spring. We're reading books now that will help Ms. Ferguson be a better teacher."

My skin crawled in a slow ripple from my toes to the top of my head.

"Look at Ms. Ferguson's face!" a student called.

Was I blushing, smiling, or bursting with anger that I try so hard to swallow down? It was just before Halloween after all, and I could have claimed that my expression was just a mask, a costume. "This is how I look when I have been used!" I could have cried and what a laugh we all would have had. Ha, ha, ha!

And then later that week, you and I talked about the next three weeks. I showed my plan, asked if I was going too fast, tried to appeal to you by saying how much you had rubbed off on me, how much I liked to whip through books. You said that you wanted them to do a book of their choice, showed me the list of possibilities.

Then, Mr. ———, you turned to the class, interrupted their latest quiz, and said: "Ms. Ferguson has a great idea for you. You'll read a free book!"

Do you think they will love me for this? Thanks, but you can leave the room now.

Shana

Dear Ms. ———,

Even though you're not the perfect teacher, even though you've been wishy-washy with your class, you were right. I think. We're a lot alike, and I know you're trying to help me get over that. It's that "Be nice, be mothering, be well liked" that our mothers or someone drilled into us the moment we were dressed in pink.

Their chatter wears away at the class, a babble of disruption that allows everyone to zone out, self-stimulate, and ignore what we are doing. They don't listen to each other or to me. Even when they seem to be paying attention, even when we went over their papers on the board, or their handouts, together, only three people turned one in. Only three people brought a draft to be peer edited. "What is this?" "What are we doing?" "What's due tomorrow?" They ask these questions as though they were not in the room, but out to lunch, out the door, floating in some other sphere of being. You reassure me that this is typical.

I sent a boy out today, Fonzi, thumbs up. During the quiz, I asked for complete silence. He chattered, mumbled, kept getting out of his chair. "Shhhh." I whispered, finger to my pursed lips. I am Snow White in a cottage full of dwarves who need a few lessons on manners. Fonzi stood and began to act like a mime. In silence, he danced, pretended he was in a box, acted the fool. Other students watched, smiled. I motioned for him to sit. He took his time.

"Do you want a referral?" I asked as I stared him straight in the eyes. I turned my back for a moment and then turned front. Fonzi clumsily hid the bird he had shown my back.

I opened my bag, pulled out the referral slips, and searched for a pen. I wrote slowly, calmly, then walked to the door.

"Good-bye," I said as he gathered his things. "See you Monday." Snow White was always a cheerful one.

At the door, Fonzi waved. "See ya."

I posted the grades so far. Half of the class is failing. The bell rang.

I knew he would go to lunch, instead of to the dean's office. I knew I had just handed him a ticket out, given him what he wanted.

After class, you came by and told me you saw another student of ours at lunch, the one who's missed most of this quarter. You've written him a referral, and I went to the dean and checked to see if Fonzi was there. I wrote another referral. I made a secret wish to my magic mirror that he will get weekend work detail.

Who's the fairest of them all?

Shana

Mr. ——,

Thanks, you sick asshole.

"Class, I'd like you to write an essay critiquing Ms. Ferguson as a teacher."

Do you honestly think you're helping me? Can't you see I'm in flames beneath this magnifying glass? Your eye, larger than God, looms over me like the mother ship from an alien planet. And they, of course, are thrilled to write yet another essay. Can't you just leave the room and let us be? I thought by the end of this year I was supposed to be in charge and you'd be slurping a Starbuck's. This isn't worth a lousy letter of recommendation.

It's funny too, those essays. I was so afraid of what they would say. But you should have been afraid. "Please don't be like Mr. ——, please don't give in to him the way you do." They don't like you either, you windbag, you old duffer. They see through your song-and-dance routine and want their money back. I wish I could be as strong as they are and tell you what I think of you. They are my master teachers, not you.

I'm enclosing their essays for you to look over. After all, it was your assignment. Please, I insist that you read them. No? Afraid of being under the magnifying glass with a class of eyes looking at you? Boo-hoo.

Ms. F.

Dear Students,

If I could start all over again, I would. Let's get rid of Mr. —— and Ms. ——, cast them out before the year even begins. Because, you see, I can't ever feel like your teacher with those two butting in all the time. I can't wear those too big, bossy shoes of Mr. ——'s or those too little slippers of Ms. ——'s. I'd rather go barefoot and risk getting splinters.

If we could start over, maybe I'd actually feel like a teacher, not a failure. Maybe you would actually learn something. It's funny how I spend so much time plotting each second I have with you, and how it never turns out the way I expect. What were you hoping would happen?

All I can say is thank you for not walking out. I guess you stayed for something. If not for me, then perhaps just to enjoy the show.

Love, Shana

SHANA FERGUSON *was a student teacher through the University of California at Berkeley's CLAD credential program. She now teaches high school English in northern California, where she has served as a master teacher herself. She also writes fiction and various forms of autobiographical pieces based on her classroom experiences.*

Olympia's Gift

Anne Holzman

Her name was Olympia, and there she stood, Black and proud and big as the mountain of the gods, reciting Maya Angelou's poem "Phenomenal Woman" at her eighth-grade graduation. A look around the room full of people dressed in Sunday clothes reminded me of my cooperating teacher's words: "For some kids, this is their last graduation. This is their last year in school." I hoped that would not be Olympia's case, but if it was, at least I was able to witness this performance.

I still enjoy returning in my mind to the gym of a middle school in one of Wisconsin's larger school districts. There's Olympia, quietly waiting beside the podium along with other students, many of them tiny by comparison. Pastel pink, blue, and yellow swirl across the shiny white field of her dress. It's almost a little-girl dress, pretty for church. Also little-girl-like are the pastel ribbons in her hair, but the hair is pressed and coifed, womanly. The whiteness of the dress sets off the blue tones in the folds of her chin; the yellows and pinks reflect her warmth and confidence. If I could paint her, the colors in her dress would also appear in her face, stroking her cheeks and heightening her magnificently wide forehead, flaring her nostrils to trumpet forth Angelou's poem.

I have dressed up a little too, but not enough to fit in with the families that surround me. Gingerly I alight on one of the plastic, fold-up benches that turn a gym into either an auditorium or a cafeteria, where a permanent potpourri of hot dogs and condiments scents the air and inspires middle school band rehearsals and dodgeball games. This room has saved the noise of countless rainy days and gives it back to these graduates now as a parting gift. I keep my fingers carefully away from the undersides of tables

13

and benches, fearful of what might have been hidden there. This much I have learned in my semester of student teaching: Don't put your hands on any surface you can't see. Little sisters in pink ruffles and lace-edged ankle socks confer between tables. Little brothers stand stiffly beside fathers and uncles, all in suits. I slouch forward on my elbows and miss a heartbeat as Olympia, approaching the podium, unfolds the paper onto which she has copied her poem.

Flashback yet further: We are in class on a morning in April. I have challenged the students to get up in front of the class and read poems. But many of them have gone to the lengths of memorizing without my direction to do so. Drawing on I can only guess what prior learning, they already know that a reading is performed best if done nearly from memory but not too much so. Most of the poems come straight off my bookshelf, and as a shy young man reads "Whitey on the Moon" from my autographed copy, I daydream about the time I bumped into the poet, Gil Scott-Heron, in a bookstore in a faraway city. The city we live in now has no published Black poets I can think of, except what the students are holding in their hands. Except in books.

It's Olympia's turn. She is a steady D student, quiet and dignified, too big for eighth grade but too good for it, too, biding her time and learning dutifully but not very fast. I have expected that she would turn down the opportunity to read and pick up extra points. But she rises. She dodges desks and chairs built for slight bodies, an icebreaking ship churning the first path through the harbor in early spring. She pulls out a book I have never seen before, a worn one passed around, shelved and unshelved, traded and opened and marked. Quietly but forcefully, she begins to read, and forms the opening line, "Pretty women wonder where my secret lies." I am thinking that Angelou wrote this poem just for Olympia. I bless the person who pulled it off a shelf and gave it to her, one of those silent helping hands that supports every teacher without either of them knowing about it. And by the final couplet, "Phenomenal woman, / That's me," I find myself wishing someone would write a poem that perfectly about me, for me.

That morning in May, I wanted a piece of Olympia's dignity, her pride, her triumph. It isn't a flattering image, but in some sense even great teachers are leeches, sucking energy from other people's success. We have few public successes of our own—in my case not even children of my own whose success I can at least claim to have had a hand in. It is no great feat for me to locate misused apostrophes, write a multiple-choice test question with only one possible answer, or even win and keep the attention of a roomful of teenagers for half an hour or so. At first it was a challenge, I admit, to get through a day (and then a week, a month, and I know of no teacher who has quite conquered the year), but what was left of it at the end to celebrate? A coffee cup not yet gone moldy, a stack of papers not yet tipped from its own weight, the closing of a zipper on a bulging briefcase. No, these tiny, private successes are plainly not enough to sustain us.

We need moments like the one I still treasure from that eighth-grade graduation. We need little miracles, moments when the rest of the community appreciates what we do every day in the classroom. We need to see that even when teaching is "only" a matter of drawing out existing talents, something we have taught a student to do makes a difference in the outside world. As Olympia stepped up to the podium, my risk in calling on students to read poetry aloud suddenly took wing and left the nest. It turned from an English teacher's romantic idiosyncrasy into a gift to all those families in the performance of a truly phenomenal young woman. Of course, no one but my students and me knew that I'd had anything to do with Olympia's performance, and for a teacher, that has to be enough. A teacher must harvest public approval privately in places like graduation ceremonies, cornering in his or her mind enough of the applause to last through the long weekend and carry into summer school and even the following fall.

The paper smoothed against her wide pastel chest, Olympia gauged her position against the height of the microphone, found it acceptable, laid the paper down, and surveyed her audience. She might have been the host at the Oscars, or a preacher at a wedding, or a senator about to launch a controversial bill. And in her own humble eighth-grade way, she was all of these, entertaining us, delivering a lesson, and challenging us to welcome her into our adult world. The rustling of little girl skirts quieted, the chatter of aunts and uncles subsided, and even the flashbulbs ceased as we all took in the moment.

ANNE HOLZMAN *student-taught in Wisconsin and has taught high school English and journalism in Wisconsin and Minnesota public schools. She lives in the Twin Cities, where she teaches in the New Voices journalism program, edits books for Redleaf Press, and is pursuing an M.F.A. in writing from Hamline University.*

Am I Necessary?
A Topic of Debate

Carla M. Panciera

Marc glances down at his feet, shifting from sneaker to sneaker. I see him in his baggy pants, his father's tie, and I understand that this is what it feels like when you don't know anything. Not that you don't know things in general, but that you don't know anything about what is happening in the present circumstance. I know this because I am a student teacher. I know this because for some reason known only to the gods of insanity, I have volunteered to coach the debate team. This is our first meet.

When someone with a scorecard says, "Begin," Marc's only hope is that someone else will speak first because he doesn't even know how to fake it. He will have to stand there with his mouth open and say, "I don't know what I'm doing." Nothing artistic or witty, just honest, something that risks another's impatience, anger, scorn, disgust—not to mention his own humiliation.

Marc in his first debate and I in my first teaching experience wish the same thing: that instead of standing before strangers admitting our ignorance, we were home under the afghan on the couch watching some sitcom we understand enough to criticize, or talking on the phone to our best friend who knows we're intelligent despite the fact that we leave the keys in the front door about once a week. In fact, we wish we were anywhere but where you can only be misunderstood.

It would be natural for Marc to despise whoever put him in this position. He might rehearse that person's slow mutilation again and again: the executioner sharpening his sickle close enough to raise the victim's neck hairs, the crowd gathering, shoving small

17

children and the elderly aside to get a clearer view, the steel shaft of a November sky framing his fantasy of revenge.

And I, with all my zeal, with all my can-do, am that object of revenge. I am the imagined figure that hunches forward, hands bound behind my back, head hung in shame, facing the hooded man who murders for a living.

Even worse, I went along to witness the debacle firsthand. I could have sat and sipped coffee in the teachers' lounge or hid in the restroom; I could have declined the advisorship in the first place. But I did none of the above. Even though I knew nothing about the activity, I said the only word I knew in those days, "Yes." The upperclassmen, desperate for an advisor, said, "No sweat, Ms. Panciera. We run things ourselves. We just need a chaperone." My older, wiser friends, in complete awareness of my incurable perfectionism, my passion for competition said, "Don't do it. You will obsess. You are not passive enough *just* to chaperone."

Those friends had vision. They predicted the pre-meet Fridays when over and over again I'd work out loud. They heard in advance the opening discussions that inevitably would wind back to whether or not government should substantially increase social services to the homeless. They anticipated the early departures I would make from social scenes ostensibly to rest up for the meet, when in actuality I faced a night of nightmares in which I would walk into the meet wearing only white socks and not recognizing any members of my team.

But this is what I saw: The brightest group of students assembled in one room motivated by something other than my teaching strategies or their class rank. Students who convinced me that without my help, their work at keeping this club alive would be wasted. And I bought it. I thought, if they can convince me to take a position I know absolutely nothing about during a time when I am nothing short of overloaded, they can argue with conviction.

Although it may not have been evident in those first few hours of the meet, my charges did argue well. They spoke well, they wrote well, and most important of all as it turns out, they bounced back well. During the morning rounds, I watched the sacrificials I sent out to scout the way for a more promising future in forensics. One pair arguing against the topic defended itself by saying the affirmative plan "made no sense." Tragically resourceful, ultimately ineffective. Another pair stopped halfway through at the request of the judge, who considered the situation hopeless enough to warrant impromptu coaching. A third pair forfeited a later round in order to step back from the onslaught and regroup. I supported their rationalization, recognizing signs of my own cowardice. I spent the afternoon being nauseous in the cafeteria, noting how every other team had brought with them boxes of files. Our table's centerpiece was a ravaged box of Wheat Thins.

And so it went that year, with me as student-teacher-slash-debate-chaperone. Due to their inherent intelligence and their instinct for survival, the team improved. They even came out ahead in one or two situations. I, however, improved very little. With so little time, with so much to learn, I defeated myself before I began. I understood how foolish I had been to add "Debate Coach" to my already extensive list of extracurriculars. I spent the year discovering where I was not needed.

For years after that experience I studied my reflection in the mirror every morning before I left for school and practiced saying, "No." No, I won't chaperone the Freshmen Semi, no I won't go to the all-night postgraduation party just to say hello, no I won't go hear your father the evangelist speak at the Ramada Inn, or ride the spirit bus to the state soccer championships (once was also enough for that). What I have chosen to do is to teach and to accept only those extracurricular activities that I have time to be good at.

I have had a few years to practice bowing out now. But other energetic, enthusiastic, crazy young teachers have taken my place at the head of activities that they believe will fold without them. And as I see these groups thrive despite my absence, I am confronted again with my own insignificance, with what lives with or without me, with how success will beat out its own path in several directions even when I am not at every corner to guide it.

CARLA M. PANCIERA *taught high school English in Burlington, Massachusetts, for ten years before taking time off to raise her three daughters. She and her husband, Dennis Donoghue, live in Rowley, Massachusetts.*

Poco a Poco

Jessica Ferrar

I arrived on Monday morning, March 19, 2001, to begin my student teaching at the Jose Vicente primary school in Tepeolulco, Mexico, a rural school about seventy miles southwest of Mexico City with a student population that is 100 percent Masawa. My assignment at this indigenous rural school was part of the BCLAD (bilingual/cross-cultural/language acquisition development) teaching credential program through California State University. I was to student teach alongside Eleazar, a Mexican student (who is also Masawa) from the Normal school in San Felipe de Progreso. When we got to the classroom, after sweeping the cement floor, we introduced ourselves to the thirty first graders, and Eleazar began his language arts lesson. I was free to walk through the classroom and work individually with the students.

I was quick to notice a young boy who sat at the far left in the first row of desks and whose name was Guadalupe. Guadalupe, along with his schoolmates, walks through fields and over mountains to get to and from school each day. He wears blue worn-out pants, black faded shoes and a red sweater that has sleeves chewed, stretched, and torn. His dark brown skin is dry, his face chapped from extensive exposure to sun and dry air. He is quiet and seems to keep himself apart from the rest of his class. He often seems to be in his own world.

Guadalupe was not getting any work done, in fact it seemed he could not read or write at all. The whole class was writing words and sentences in their notebooks while Guadalupe sat at his desk and stared at the blank page. I went over to help him and he would not look at me, acknowledge me, or respond in any way. I thought that perhaps it was a cultural thing—that maybe Masawa children don't look into the eyes of their teachers. I didn't push him to look at me or respond, but I was persistent and consistent in going over to him to scaffold his learning and help him get on task. Guadalupe hadn't even begun to write his name on his paper. I told him to write his name and the date (which was on the board) and that I would be back to see it shortly. When I returned he was looking off into space and still hadn't written a thing. I felt stumped. What can I do to help? I wondered. I felt like there was a wall between us, as if he didn't hear me or understand me, and he never once looked up at me, he kept his eyes fixed on his desk.

I began to feel a strong desire to help Guadalupe. I made sure to pass by his seat every few minutes to encourage him to write. I soon realized he was not going to do any work on his own so I wrote the information for him on a separate piece of paper so he could copy it in his notebook. When I returned to see how he was doing, he had done it. Written in his notebook was: Guadalupe Jose Alvaro 19 de Marzo, 2001.

"Excelente, Guadalupe," I told him. "Now let's write a sentence." He dictated. I wrote what he said on a piece of paper. He copied it into his notebook. I was thrilled. Progress! Even if it was copying my writing, he was at least forming letters and using his pencil.

This went on for the whole week. Guadalupe would tune out, sit and do nothing during class. I would approach him; he wouldn't look at me, talk to me, or respond to my questions. I would write out what he needed to write, or tell him letter by letter and he would slowly get that small task done—but only if I was right there to check up on him. I continued to contemplate Guadalupe's situation. Why was it so hard for him to follow directions? Why did he need constant guidance? Why wouldn't he relate to me? Something about his apparent isolation touched me. I consistently went to his side to help him. Then, the following week, while I was standing by the window near Guadalupe's desk, I put a throat lozenge in my mouth. Suddenly I heard Guadalupe say,

"Dame un dulce! Give me a candy!" He was looking right up at me, demanding I share with him. I told him that it wasn't candy, that it was for my throat. But inside I was shouting, "Yes! You go Guadalupe!" Sure, he didn't even say please, and ought not to boss his teacher around, but I was thrilled that he was opening up and comfortable enough to ask me, or command me rather, to share. In that moment I realized that all the small efforts I had made, all of those moments that I had to call upon my patience in order to stay with Guadalupe to see him succeed in even the smallest way, had paid off and that he was beginning to feel safe with me. I realized how essential it was that Guadalupe trust me and feel secure with me for him to engage in learning.

Things just took off from there. Guadalupe and I began to work and learn together. He let me guide and encourage him and he started to stay on task. One time he even got out of his seat, came over to me with his notebook, held it up to my face, and without words asked with a questioning look in his eyes, "Is this right?" I couldn't believe it. This was the boy who a week ago wouldn't even write his name. This was the first grader who would not look up or respond to me in any way. "Yes! Guadalupe," I said, fighting back tears of pride and satisfaction. "Yes! That's right. You've got it! Adelante!"

It's moments like these with Guadalupe that make teaching such a rewarding profession. By the end of my two weeks of student teaching in that classroom, Guadalupe was writing his own list of words: *gato, rana, nubes*. The assignment was to write the names of objects he saw behind a picture of a cow, but he couldn't contain himself, he wrote words for everything he saw in front, behind, to the left and to the right of that cow and even a few extra words that came to mind!

Those two weeks with Guadalupe, although brief, represent for me the beauty of the student-teacher relationship. As every teachers says, it is a reciprocal learning experience, and often it is our students who are our greatest teachers. Guadalupe taught me patience, faith, and the importance of taking things poco a poco—one step at a time.

JESSICA FERRAR *is a native New Yorker who has lived in the San Francisco Bay Area for the last eleven years. She holds a degree in interdisciplinary studies from UC Berkeley, has worked with children in classrooms, has taught creative dance for children, teaches yoga, and passionately loves to dance. She recently returned from a ten-month stay in Queretaro, Mexico, where she studied and student-taught as part of her bilingual multiple-subject teaching credential through Cal State University. She recently completed her student teaching in a bilingual classroom in San Diego, California, and graduated at the end of June 2001.*

Mission to Mars

An Excerpt from My Student Teaching Journal

Ainslie Cole

Student teaching. Equivalent to a Mormon mission? As humbling as the road to Mecca? Actually, nothing compares—well, maybe a mission to Mars! I never expected teaching to be like this. I thought I had it licked when I could get a group of seventh- and eighth-grade English language learners to write haiku poetry utilizing similes, metaphors, and onomatopoeia. Naive as that was, I also thought that my student teaching would be a whizzzzzzzz.

I began teaching this week with my second grade *angels* . . . and I use the term loosely. These little manipulators have a greater effect on human emotion than Prozac. One minute, I'm a confident student teacher, buzzing with ideas and making connections; the next minute, as Juan Carlos and Hugo play sword fight with shards of glass they found in the yard, I find myself facing the obvious question: *What am I doing here? I'm not made for this!!!!!* To be honest, I'm a big sissy. I can't handle the fast lane with my sister in the driver's seat, and I certainly can't survive the ups and downs of second grade. But is it normal for a teacher to look the other way when Santiago is teaching us how to play leapfrog . . . from tabletop to tabletop? It's amazing what they get away with. I can remember back to elementary school when I thought I was going to be sent home for *sharpening my pencil* while Sister Breege Boyle explained an activity! The name alone sent chills down my spine. When she put the fear of God in me—combined with the fear of my mother's face should I *ever* get sent home—I was the last one to swing from the lights.

Teachers are the most incredible people in the world. I truly think they should be the ones to interview politicians, or conduct

25

parole hearings, or sit in on confessions. *Nobody* can do what teachers do. Hissy fits, lies, deception, and down-right *bribery* (as we all have a collection of apples) are tried and tested on a daily basis. Teachers have to deal with the world's greatest con artists *every single day!* And somehow, they do it. They manage a classroom full of eager and energetic bodies, captivating them with knowledge and stretching their imaginations. They produce doctors, priests, CEOs, and presidents . . . even the next generations of teachers.

I've learned to ignore little Luis when he runs along the windows demonstrating his version of "the bird," and instead focus on the lesson at hand. I cherish the memories I have of elementary school, when time wasn't an issue, and losing recess *was* the end of the world. Now I just hope I get through this adventure as smoothly as Gulliver and Ulysses did . . . and keep my two eyes and teeth intact in the meantime.

As a little girl, AINSLIE COLE gave her first math lesson to a room full of stuffed animals. Her pigtails and overalls were a mere disguise for her natural love of teaching. She currently teaches a bilingual third grade in Las Vegas, still disguised in pigtails and overalls, spreading the fun of learning.

Chiffon Bit the Para

Barbara Tramonte

The school assignment came unexpectedly. I was due at Avenue N and East Fifty-third Street in Brooklyn at 8:00 A.M. the next day. My first ten-week residency as a poet in the New York City schools was about to begin. I should've gotten more notice, but Jean LeCour, the poet originally slotted for the assignment, had gotten lucky and was named poet laureate of Brooklyn the week before. Struck suddenly with stardom (and a generous salary of $1.00 per year) Jean decided to opt out of his teaching assignment and do a series of readings at city hall. The following morning I left my neighborhood in Brooklyn Heights and sped down the vibrating Brooklyn Queens Expressway, huge trucks rattling on either side of me, headed for P.S. 192.

I was nervous. A new school. Pepto Bismol and my belief in poetry as an educational emancipator propelled me forward. That, and the expectation of the shining faces of the children I was going to teach.

I careened onto Avenue N, passing mundane rows of houses signaling the outer boroughs. There was plenty of sky and an abundance of mothers pushing strollers or holding children's hands in this neighborhood. I swung my car into a parking space in front of the school behind the designated handicapped parking spot. A yellow van was emitting children using walkers, in wheelchairs, and on crutches into the building. In they went—into the cavernous reality of a New York City public school—just in time to hear the drone of the principal's voice over the P.A. system, "Good mawning, girls and boys. Mustafa will lead us in the pledge today. And congratulations to class 3-325 for perfect attendance this month. Mustafa . . ."

A squeaky voice sputtered over the loudspeakers as people everywhere—in corridors, in classrooms, and in stairwells—stopped to recite the pledge. I flung my right hand across my chest and recited, audibly, "And to the Republic for which it stands, one nation, under God, indivisible, with liberty and justice for all." It might as well have been 1956, me in a starched middy blouse with a hanky pinned to my chest. My brothers and sisters and I always had our nails clean, our dental notes in on time, and our shoes polished. Teachers in Brooklyn used to walk down the straight rows of desks daily to see whether our hygiene was up to snuff and then mark their findings in a little blue soft-covered book. The results found their way onto our yellow report cards each quarter.

I checked my sheet. Room 202. When I walked in, Mrs. Marmelman was at the front of the room gently pushing two boys away while screaming in a copper-plated Brooklyn blast, "I said back to yaw seats." When the class quieted down she raised both hands like Moses parting the Red Sea. "This is Mrs. Tramonte, boys and girls. She has come a long way to be with you and she has something very special to teach you." All eyes, like twinkling wire-strung lights, flashed toward me. Then Mrs. Marmelman walked in front of her desk and opened her hands in an imaginary embrace, and said, "You were chosen from all the third-grade classes to be taught poetry." Never mind that the third grade contained only two classes. This class believed that they were chosen by a higher power to be taught poetry and they straightened in their seats like cartoon flowers hankering for the sun. I started to feel calm and positive about who I was and why I was there. I stepped into my role like softener in the dryer. The class was going to feel good now.

I began my lesson by calling three volunteers to the front of the room. I spoke about making writing come alive. "How do we describe things?" I planted my hands firmly on one girl's shoulders and twirled her so she faced the class. "If I say Tamika has brown eyes. Boring!" And I yawned. The class giggled predictably. "But if I say

Tamika has eyes as brown as . . . ," and here I paused dramatically seeming to search for the right word. A voice from the front yelled, "Chocolate." Yes, I smiled my kindly teacher smile, "Tamika has eyes as brown as chocolate," "What else could Tamika's eyes be like?" From the back row came a shout, "A bear." We were on our way to thinking in comparisons, forging connections, and building smiles.

After my brief motivational presentation the children were hopping to write. Brian had problems and was isolated in the back far corner of the room. Some children said they couldn't think of anything to write. Others burned their papers with an endless stream of molten lead. There was no stopgap for them between thought and expression. It was all go, go, go. Others could only write about Tomb Raider, or the Rugrats, or Britney Spears. Brian threw a chair at Bagdalena. Mrs. Marmelman shouted, "Brian. Get out! Go to the principal's office. I'm calling your aunt today!"

Shevaud, unusually large for his age, just snickered and declined to write. Caryl, a pale West Indian boy, wrote a barrage of bizarre symbols vaguely resembling hieroglyphs. The writing session meandered through the morning punctuated by the rustles of arms being raised and hands desperately clawing the air for attention. "Mrs. Tramonte, Mrs. Tramonte," they called with the urgency of someone with a full bladder. As I traversed the room, bending down to meet their tiny heads and ask what I might offer, I was greeted by varied requests for help. "How do you spell shopping mall?" Chris asked. "How do you spell Super Nintendo?" Lacey pleaded. Charles beckoned with the "Oooh, Oooh, Oooh" of a quiz-show participant.

"Can I say my grandma's a mean witch?" Sarayah pleaded. I felt mixed. I knew what the administration was looking for, and yet I fiercely believed in freedom of expression. Should I give the kids a taste of real freedom?

"Your grandma's not mean!" thundered Mrs. Marmelman.

"Yes," I nodded kindly. "You can say your grandma's mean."

All the while Mrs. Marmelman roamed the room overseeing students' writing as she bent over desk after desk. "Come on, Betty. Write something!" she growled.

"But I can't think of anything," Betty pleaded.

"Write about the blue sky," Mrs. Marmelman prodded. "Say the sky is as blue as powder," Mrs. Marmelman continued pointed to examples on the board.

Betty just wriggled in her seat. Mrs. Marmelman pointed to the lines I had written on the board, meant purely as a kick-off point. "Look at what Mrs. Tramonte wrote on the board," Mrs. Marmelman shrieked hysterically, "And copy them."

A small girl with a gold-threaded scarf wrapped Bedouin-style around her head raised her hand meekly. I strode to the back of the room and leaned over her desk.

"Can I write about coffeepot?"

"Yes. Yes. What will you say about coffeepot, Salumia?"

"Coffeepot push coffee pearls like string talk." I was stunned. This little girl with hardly any English configured words with the graceful leap of a Chagall painting.

Mrs. Marmelman cornered me while the children wrote. "Shevaud's mother's on crack. He's been held back," she said. "Caryl's new. He just came from Haiti. He saw his mother and father shot in front of him. First he lived with an aunt in Queens. Now his grandma took him in. Betty can't control herself. Their parents don't care about them. That's how these people are."

I felt the surge of racism that snakes around so many U.S. classrooms with its biting venom. I'd seen it before. I'd met it head on in almost every teacher's lunchroom in New York City. "These kids can't learn. They don't know any better."

Ten minutes left. Time for sharing poems—only by those who were willing. Chris got up and read a long boring poem about Nintendo and girlfriends and Lamborghinis. Third-grade urban boys love Lamborghinis and other souped-up cars. Melinda Johnstone, a perky blonde with green eyes and rhinestones on her shirt, read about rainbows, unicorns, and the "sun that loves us all." Mrs. Marmelman was brought to tears. "That was beautiful, Melinda."

Caryl reluctantly got up and read a hip-hoppy verse that went like this:

> Kit Kat and Kangaroo
> Catch kings and cricket creepers.
> Come back!

Mrs. Marmelman let me know that Caryl had never spoken before or let on that he could read or write. I felt the noose loosen for Caryl. If only for these thirty-five minutes, poetry set him free in a Brooklyn classroom.

Fergus got up and spoke of his wish that his "dad return from the dead like a cool wind through the door."

I floated on the unlocked love these kids unfurled in this little Brooklyn classroom in this corner of the world and, for a few minutes, my own worries—the tax man, my children, the crime and poverty in New York—meant nothing to me.

I moved through the halls to Mrs. O'Connell's class 2-419, and as I walked in, Mrs. O'Connell, a Brillo box with blonde hair, was shouting, "Chiffon bit the para! Chiffon bit the para!" The paraprofessional was exiting the room clutching her arm as Mrs. O'Connell lunged toward me holding a small girl by her puffed sleeve. The girl, with rows of tightly woven braids plastered flat on her head, smiled at no one in particular. This must be Chiffon, I thought. Mrs. O'Connell exhorted me to watch the class as she ushered the small girl from the room. I stood helplessly in front of thirty-two writhing, overexcited fourth graders who were bouncing off desks and throwing things.

"All right, calm down," I screamed. The Pepto Bismol had worn off and a creeping acidic river inched its way into my lower belly. There was no response. A good-looking boy with a wide smile pulled a good-looking girl-with-wide-eyes' hair. "Ouch," she screamed, but her curved smile emitted her pleasure like a radiant perfume. I put my books down and stood back against the blackboard. I surveyed the boisterous group of nine- and ten-year-old players before me. I hesitated. Should I attempt to quiet them? It seemed impossible.

Two girls with braids and small, plastic, bubble-bath bottles strung around their necks approached me. "Hi, are you the new poetry teacher?" They fingered my scarf and let me know they thought I was pretty. "Mrs. O'Connell's gonna kill us," one said with her gapped teeth smiling perfect innocence. Eamon, a big boy wearing a red and yellow Stone Cold Steve Austin shirt pulled the chair from under Quigley, a small boy with motor-skill problems. Quigley landed flat on his ass and began to cry. A boy who barely spoke English and appeared to be Russian laughed and said "nyet" quite loudly. One of the braided, bubbly girls was stroking my very straight hair and said, "That's Tom. He just got here from Russia. He doesn't know any English."

I screamed at the class with all the force I suddenly felt build up like steam inside me. I knew I had to quiet them or someone would get hurt. "I will send you to Mrs. Paratzzi's office if you don't settle down!" I yelled. "Everybody in your seats!" The majority of the children immediately popped into my reality and heard me screaming. They began to settle into their seats. Several still cavorted, stealing each other's pens and shouting taunts.

"I SAID TAKE YOUR SEATS!" I screamed.

"Where should I take it?" Eamon guffawed.

Suddenly the bulwark, the Brillo box, the battleship, Mrs. O'Connell, marched into the room. She clicked the light switch on and off several times. That old teacherly trick. Why hadn't I thought of that? Children flopped like rag dolls into their seats. "HEADS ON DESKS!" Mrs. O'Connell cracked. I stood watching incredulously as all heads dropped down onto the desks like brain prisoners in an institution for unwieldy thought. While the children's heads lay quietly on their desks, Mrs. O'Connell shouted with the gutter rippling through her voice, "Keisha! Come here." A girl dressed in tatters slowly lifted her head and blinked her eyes. She raised her frail body from the seat. I noticed an odd long scar on her calf. It was a keloid, pink as the inside of a bunny's ear, on her long dark leg. Mrs. O'Connell got very close to Keisha's ear. She shouted with the unleashed force of a water hose out of control. "You did not bring me your homework again today. Tell

32

your grandmother I want a note from her. Why didn't you do your homework?"

Keisha looked lost, like a scared fox in the forest. She twittered nervously and looked to the floor. Mrs. O'Connell bent over and pumped up the volume. "WHY DIDN'T YOU DO YOUR WORK LAST NIGHT, KEISHA?" The girl was near tears and looked the other way. Finally, Mrs. O'Connell let up. She turned Keisha around and sent her back to her desk. She walked over to me and said, "Hi. You must be Barbara Tramonte. I'm Barb O'Connell." Then, nodding toward Keisha, she said louder than I would have liked, "Her mother just died of AIDS and her grandma has to keep her. It's a pity the way she dresses."

I felt something inside me swoon at this display. I looked over at the little girl and smiled a tender smile. Keisha smiled with a shy, uplifted gaze. She seemed bathed in a pool of light, like a princess. I began my second poetry lesson of the day with squelched, mixed feelings. I was operating on all levels, like a multitiered urban mall. Even as I spoke, explaining similes, breathing life into wishes, exploring feelings, Mrs. O'Connell screamed, ignoring all goings-on, displaying the awareness of a Plexiglas shield between passenger and driver in a New York City cab.

At one point Mrs. O'Connell screeched, "Audley, get up here." When little Audley toddled to the front of the room, Mrs. O'Connell grabbed his face and cupped it between her hands. She titled it to the ceiling. "Do you have conjunctivitis? Is that conjunctivitis? Go to the nurse now!" As Audley exited the room Barb O'Connell turned to me and said, "How could his mother send him to school like that?"

When the class was over I found my way to a pay phone and dialed my husband, Bob, at the children's bookshop we owned in Brooklyn Heights. "Runaway Bunny." His voice was jolly. He always said retail was theatre. It was all an act.

"Bob. It's me."

"Honey bunny one-y." He was the embodiment of optimism. "Here, someone wants to speak to you." Before I could make my groan audible a voice I barely recognized was on the other end,

"Hello, Barbar-a how are you? Do you know who this is?" I knew. It was Pria, a neighbor from long ago. Bob and I hadn't seen her for a while.

"It is Pria," she intoned in her lilting accent. I liked Pria. She was an English professor at Queens College. She was bright, nice-looking, always in a sari, and she smoked Gauloises. But I didn't feel like talking to Pria right now. "I am discussing with your delightful husband the ins and outs of lit-rary biography."

"How wonderful," I tried to sound genuine.

"I am hoping we can see each other soon. Asad is working on translating some new Urdu poetry and would like very much to read some to you and Bob."

"We'd love it." I heard the gonglike bell vibrate through the school and knew I was due at my next class. Bob got on for one split second and said, "OK, hon. I've got to go." I hung up the phone feeling so needy. As needy as Keisha. As tattered as Keisha. As abandoned. But this only lasted one nanosecond. I knew my husband loved me and I was too frazzled to entertain another thought.

My next class was Mrs. Blauberg's "gifted" fifth grade, which I found very dull. The children were filled with flat ideas expressed with sterling, sparkling enthusiasm. Both class and teacher were inordinately enamored of Haiku and Tanka verse and spent count-less gelatinous moments squeezing their thoughts into the ready-made rigidity of the form. Mrs. Blauberg even knew of a Haiku contest sponsored by Japan Air Lines and asked me to prep the class to enter. I groaned as I thought of yet another honor bestowed on this bunch. As far as I could tell, they were only endowed with material advantage. Most of the children in Mrs. Blauberg's fifth-grade class were White.

After a mealy, miserable lunch in the teacher's lunchroom dis-cussing best bargain malls and one teacher's foray into private pyramid underwear sales, I steeled myself for my last class. Some-thing I was no longer looking forward to.

I left P.S. 192 with warring emotions. I loved teaching these kids, but I couldn't stand the tipped scales of privilege and disadvantage accompanied by the maddening pretense that none of it exists. I boogeyed to my waiting, parked, dirty Toyota. I affectionately referred to my car as "a garbage can on wheels." The radio had been ripped out and hopeless colored wires dangled where good music used to be. I sped to the highway and curved toward the bookstore and Brooklyn Heights. The brownstones and Federal-style houses were a relief in their architectural civility after the squat saltboxes of Marine Park. I double-parked in front of the store with my hazard lights flashing and dashed into the crowded, bustling room. I reached over the counter and kissed Bob on the cheek just as a brown-suited meter maid slapped a $25 fine on my windshield.

"Goddamn it, Bob, I was only out of the car for two seconds."

"Barbara. Barbara. You know you love it."

Bob's eyes twinkled as the day reeled through my head. Those beautiful children at their desks at P.S. 192, filled with so much love and curiosity. The cramped shop filled with children's books and parents, toddlers, and strollers. I turned to look at Bob and smiled.

"Gridlock discount. Gridlock discount," he shouted as two ladies with baby carriages tried in vain to struggle through the narrow entry to the store. I had one foot out the door, yelling at the meter maid, "OK, OK, I'm movin' it."

BARBARA TRAMONTE *is a published poet and teacher living in Amherst, Massachusetts.*

Best and Brightest

Jorge Verlenden

I'm thirty-four. I have worked for a multinational software developer. I have studied Arabic and Greek and French. I have hiked mountains and traveled by bus through the Middle East. I have lived abroad and taught young Sudanese refugees English, this last experience leading me to teaching. I received a master's degree in elementary education, with a specialty in reading. I won the graduate school award.

One would think that such a person as described above—worldly, educated, somewhat of a workaholic—would have no trouble skating through the first year of teaching twenty-one first graders. Indeed certain educational reformers claim that in order to solve our country's educational woes, we simply need to hire intelligent, experienced individuals. Since I saw myself as part of the "best and brightest" contingent, I believed that approach myself. Such idealism, along with my experiences in the Middle East, were what led me to incur a grossly inflated debt for higher education and abandon a lucrative career in the dot-com world.

I think of the *Atlantic Monthly* article that I referenced in my grad school application essay. In it, Paul Gagnon (1995) complains that educators have been "unable to conceive of excellence and equity co-existing in the schools most children have to attend" (65). He goes on to call citizens to the difficult chore of content-based reform. I felt up to Gagnon's challenge and believed that I possessed the peculiar talent the educational world needed.

In grad school my professors called for similar reform. They addressed us as if we were passionate knights bearing light and reason. Unfortunately I was all too willing to see myself as this knight. As a result, I failed to understand the juggling acts performed by

36

teachers and the demands of the bureaucratic tangle that is also education.

But on August 4, 2000, the day after my Lufthansa flight from Amman touched down in New Orleans, I formally began my first year of teaching. I soon realized that being a good teacher was a little more complicated than I had thought. That morning I was scheduled to meet with the principal, the curriculum director, my first-grade colleagues, and a parent volunteer to discuss my future class and to review my duties and their expectations. After that first meeting, my notes contained fifty-six equally important entries including:

> Twenty-one children with IQs ranging from 90 to 155.
> Four children with severe learning disabilities.
> Reticent parents.
> Two well-known bullies.
> Extend the gifted and pull up the strugglers.
> Integrate technology and design a Web page.
> Implement new findings about the teaching of reading, writing, and mathematics.
> Plan lessons in five- to fifteen-minute increments.
> Offer engaging, child-centered yet teacher-directed activities.
> Integrate real-world issues into the classroom environment.
> Don't scare the children.
> Stay within budget.
> Field 10 p.m. complaint calls with diplomacy.
> Smile and laugh.

The curriculum director closed our meeting with an encouraging comment, "This is your first year. We know there's a lot of pressure. We aren't asking for perfection or a star performance. We just want you to be organized and to follow through on your basic duties as we've explained them."

I nodded. On the outside I must have looked young, smart, and fashionable. On the inside I was overwhelmed, near tears. I wondered to myself how to address the needs of the children reading fifth-grade novels. I worried about the young boy whose parents considered his learning disability to be his fault. I tried to imagine the play that I had to write for my students to perform.

I returned to my classroom, which, because a summer camp had used the facilities, was in total disrepair. As I pushed around chairs and tore off bulletin-board paper, I gave myself confidence-boosting messages. However, they were of the mean-spirited, defensive variety that seem to come out when there's a sense of impending failure. I thought, "If those pathetically dressed dusty old marms can get it together, surely I can. I'm a risk taker, a reformer. They'll be coming to me for advice quite soon."

Empty puffery. Three days before the opening of school, the near-tears turned to real ones. My room was still a shambles. I'd yet to finalize my teaching plans for the opening week. I felt nervous, edgy, angry. I was sure I was coming across as scattered, obsessive, and maniacal. I feared that not only had my confidence been shaken but that others could see this fact all too clearly.

A sweetly smiling, alarmingly calm kindergarten teacher poked her head into my doorway. "How are you doing?" she said. When I couldn't answer right away, for fear of breaking down, she quickly said, "How about a little help?"

She ducked out of the entryway, back into the hall and before I could wonder what she was up to, she'd returned with four of my colleagues.

They were clad in child-friendly T-shirts adorned with teddy bears and fuzzy appliqués. Yarn dangled from sleeves and shirttails. *Pathetically dressed.* "Let's see, where shall we start?" one of the ladies said. The four women began to move about my room. One of them began a friendly conversation about movies and lunch. The discussion turned into one on teaching philosophy. They talked about how to reconcile systematic instruction with inquiry-based learning. One person mentioned one of my learning disabled students. She suggested I consult Mel Levin's work and bookmarked a website on my computer. They pushed furniture, arranged the art and writing centers, added erasers and stickers to pencil boxes. They cut bulletin-board trim and stapled it up. They discussed my opening-day plans, explained car pool duties and what to do if I needed to go to the bathroom during the day. I'd forgotten such departures from the classroom had to be planned.

At some point the curriculum director popped in. "Are you ready?" she said, looking at me. Before I could respond, one of the ladies said, "She's fine. Almost set. We just stopped by to moon over all her progress. She's going to have a great year." The administrator raised her eyebrows and disappeared into the hallway. The ladies looked at me with conspiratorial smiles. Had I thought I'd known these people? When they left that day, my classroom had taken on a sense of calm and order. So had I.

"You've got to ask a lot of questions," one of them later advised. "The first year can be overwhelming. At times you might not feel you'll make it through. But remember, we're here to help." I reconsidered my judgment of their fashion choices. I began to realize that my best and brightest image might not be so realistic.

But this lesson, too, I had to learn by experience. On the first day of school I sported a fuchsia silk wraparound skirt and a pair of black and gray funky boots. My colleagues dressed in flashy, comfy clothes, adorned with gilded parrots, fuzzy teddy bears, and love bugs. Although I struggled to keep my skirt closed while sitting on the floor or lifting little bodies to the monkey bars, the day was successful for all of us. When the bell rang at 3:00, I led my entourage of small, excited students out to car pool, while retaining the edgy look that made me personally feel like the best and brightest.

It was a beautiful New Orleans afternoon. Overcast skies and a deep gulf breeze kept the air cool. I waved to parents, closed car doors, lifted backpacks. Suddenly someone realized a child was missing—one of my students. I was asked to run the distance of the playground to the other car pool where the older elementary children waited. When I took off down the sidewalk, a looping gust reached under my hemline and scooped the skirt into the air. The split that occasionally exposed my thigh now revealed my green panties with their yellow flower buds. I jerked my skirt closed, but the tugging and pulling loosened the snazzy rosette knot tied around my waist. The skirt came open from the top, revealing my underwear again. I stopped to rewrap and tied my garment, but by this time the car pool began honking. Parents waved, smiled. One of my helpers from the previous days rushed up smiling, "I should have told you: never wear a wraparound."

"I'm learning," I said and raced off to look for my missing child.

Gagnon, Paul. 1995. "What Should Children Learn?" *Atlantic Monthly* 256 (6): 65–78.

JORGE VERLENDEN *teaches first grade at Isidore Newman School in New Orleans, Louisiana. She has an M.S. in elementary education from Loyola University and is embarking on her second year of full-time classroom teaching.*

Give Me a B

Carol Schwalberg

Even before I stepped into the cubicle, Yetta Isaacs was ready to learn. She sat bolt upright, her wrinkled hands splayed across the primer, holding it open to the place.

I was itching to know why the dressmaker had waited so many years to start her studies—in the twenties everyone might have worn those low-heeled black oxfords, but now in 1948, no one under fifty thought of buying them—but Mr. Cohen wouldn't like me to pry. Instead of getting to the point, I asked, "How did you hear of the Eastern Institute?"

Mrs. Isaacs' pale blue eyes widened behind her bifocals. "My neighbor told me. An ad in the *Freiheit*. You know the ad?"

"No" was the wrong answer because Mr. Cohen never wanted the pupils to find out that the tutors, all college girls like me, had no Yiddish and couldn't read a Yiddish newspaper. He told us, "Any time a student wishes to converse in Yiddish, place a finger upon your lips and say, 'We speak English here.'"

Mr. Cohen had translated the primer into Yiddish and then transliterated the Yiddish into English characters, slipping the pages into loose-leaf notebooks, which the tutors held beneath the worktables where the students couldn't see.

"We'd better get on with our work," I said.

Mr. Cohen passed the cubicle right then and smiled approvingly. "Don't waste the student's time," he always said. I wanted to stay on good terms with him. The job paid seventy cents an hour and kept me busy ten hours a week.

As Mrs. Isaacs read each sentence, I was careful to slip her forefinger down the notebook, line for line. Once I'd lost her place, and when the student asked the meaning of "He left the house," I said, "Die maydels klayde," the girl's dress.

While the tutors worked in their cubicles, Mr. Cohen kept the books and signed up students from behind his large desk stained the same gloomy dark oak as the instructors' tables. The walls of his office, painted an institutional light green like the rest of the Eastern Institute, had only one decoration, a large reproduction of the Declaration of Independence.

"You're quite patriotic," I said during the first interview. The slim man looked at me sharply from behind his steel-rimmed glasses, fastened the top button of his dark gray suit and continued to quiz me on uses of the conditional.

After hiring me, he said, "As a young immigrant, I studied accounting and English in night school. I did well, but many others did not. The problem lay in the classes. The brighter students could not move ahead quickly and the slower ones needed additional assistance. I decided to establish a school where students received individual attention. I chose the location carefully. Times Square—"

I thought of the whores, winos, and pickpockets ten stories below and burst out, "But all the riffraff!"

The man nodded sagely, "Yes, but Eastern Institute is easy to reach. No matter which subway the student uses, all lines stop at Forty-second Street."

I had been tutoring Mrs. Isaacs for seven weeks, and the woman was still struggling through the chapter where Mrs. Smith sent her son Tommy to the market. Putting a finger under each word, Mrs. Isaacs bent over the book and read from the list "...corn, bread..." She looked up. "The boy buys bread in a grocery? That rotten white bread I wouldn't give an enemy? They must be goyim."

I stifled a laugh and tapped the text. "Just keep on reading."

Mrs. Isaacs bent closer to the book. "Milk, raisins, bah-con—"

"Stop there. The word is bacon."

"Bacon," Mrs. Isaacs repeated.

"Do you know what bacon is?" I said. Mrs. Isaacs nodded. I pushed back from the table. "Use the word in a sentence."

Mrs. Isaacs screwed up her face in concentration. "I'm bakin' the bread."

I bit my lip. "That's not right. Are you sure you know what bacon is?" Mrs. Isaacs shook her head. I crouched over the table and whispered, "Pork."

"Aha! I knew it. Goyim." Mrs. Isaacs looked triumphant. I pointed to the book. Mrs. Isaacs shrugged. "So okay, the little shaygetz shops for his mother. He's a good boy. Like my son." She fumbled in her purse, brought out a tired black leather wallet and flipped it open to a snapshot. "Here."

I glanced at a picture of a man in his early thirties with what I supposed was his wife and two children and pointed to the book again. "Nice. Let's read."

Two weeks later, Mrs. Isaacs was still stumbling through the shopping list. Why couldn't the woman learn? She wasn't stupid. I went to the college library and consulted books on teaching slow readers.

The next time Mrs. Isaacs came into the Eastern Institute, I waited until Mr. Cohen, pale and perspiring, rushed to the men's room down the hall, put her hands over the primer and told the older woman, "I think you'd do better with another text. Ask your son to go to the library and borrow a reader about adults living in the city."

Several reminders later, Mrs. Isaacs brought in a primer that mirrored New York life, but she still inched ahead, learning little from one lesson to the next. In the meantime, enrollment at the Eastern Institute slumped, and my work week dropped from ten hours to five. I needed more pocket money.

The next time Mrs. Isaacs came in for her lesson, I waited until Mr. Cohen rushed to the men's room before saying, "You're not learning."

The older woman drew back. "I need you to tell me I'm not learning? I know."

"But you can."

Mrs. Isaacs shook her head. "My grandson Jeffrey, he can learn. He's only six and already he's reading better than me, and I'm fifty-seven," She sighed. "That's why I started here. Jeffrey shouldn't think his bubbe is a dummy."

"All you need is a different method," I assured her.

"No, I'm a dummy. Mr. Cohen made up the method, and he's an educated man. He showed me his diploma."

"What diploma?"

"You haven't seen the one on the wall behind his desk?"

So that's why Mr. Cohen put up the Declaration of Independence. "You're not a dummy. You just need a different technique, but Mr. Cohen won't let me use one."

Mrs. Isaacs drew back. "So what can I do?"

"Let me teach you privately. In your own home. You won't need to make the long trip from the Bronx to Forty-second Street."

"No shlepping from the Bronx. Hm."

I warmed to the attack. "It will cost less money."

Mrs. Isaacs leaned forward. "How less money?"

"Here you pay seven dollars an hour. I'll charge only five."

Mrs. Isaacs drew a worn piece of paper from her purse. "My address for you to copy. Take the Pelham train to Elder Avenue. When you're on the street and want to find my house, ask. Someone will tell. Come next Thursday at four."

I was thrilled. I would earn more money in two hours with Mrs. Isaacs than in ten at the Eastern Institute.

We met in the kitchen. Mrs. Isaacs gestured to a plate of cookies on the table. "Take. From my house, no one should go hungry."

I bit into a cookie. "Delicious. Now let's get to work. What do you want to do?"

"Enough with Tommy and white bread. I want to write the cleaning woman she shouldn't come." I must have looked perplexed for Mrs. Isaacs continued, "I don't have so many customers I couldn't clean."

"Why don't you just tell her not to come any more?"

"Say it to her face? I couldn't. She's a nice woman. Working for me five years."

I tore a sheet of paper from her notebook. "Let's begin with the date."

Mrs. Isaacs rummaged in a cupboard drawer and came up with a pencil. She looked at me expectantly. "The date," I said, tapping the paper.

"So what's the date?"

"March 30."

"How do I write March?"

I said, "You begin with a capital *m*, then you write a-r-c-h." Mrs. Isaacs sat motionless. "You do remember how to form an *m*, don't you?" I said.

"Remind me."

I took up the pencil and, using my best Palmer script, formed the letter. "Now you do it." I pushed the paper back to Mrs. Isaacs.

The dressmaker picked up the pencil and, breathing heavily, copied the letter. When she was finished, she handed the paper back to me.

"This is an *n*, Mrs. Isaacs. One hill. See, there are two hills in the *m* I made. You have to add another hill."

Once again Mrs. Isaacs took up the pencil. Looking constantly at my example, she slowly shaped the letter. "There. Two hills."

"Good. Now you have to write an *a*."

"I forget."

I wrote out the *a*, and Mrs. Isaacs copied it. By the time the hour was up, we had gone no further than the date. I told her to practice until the next lesson.

The next week Mrs. Isaacs brought out a blank sheet of paper and, looking confident, began to write March 30. I held her hand. "The date is now April 4."

"I can't write March 30?" Mrs. Isaacs said. I shook my head. "Oy vey. So learn me April 4."

"You remember how to make an *a*, don't you?" Mrs. Isaacs sighed. "You think you don't, but you do." I pointed to the *a* in March. "See? Here's an *a*. Now write the *a* for me."

Mrs. Isaacs began breathing heavily. Glancing at the date she had written earlier, she slowly drew a lowercase *a*.

"That's a small *a*. April is a proper noun, the name of a month." Mrs. Isaacs frowned. "We need a capital." I demonstrated.

Mrs. Isaacs formed a capital *a*. "So now?"

I wrote out the rest of the date. Mrs. Isaacs spent the remaining time copying it.

At the next lesson I had only to demonstrate a 6, and the date was complete. "Now for the letter itself. First, we write *Dear*. You do remember how, don't you?"

Mrs. Isaacs sat motionless. I didn't wait for her to say that she didn't, but traced the letters onto the page. Mrs. Isaacs copied the letters and promised to practice.

I was happy to leave. These lessons with Mrs. Isaacs were trying. She seemed to learn so slowly. There must be a better way to teach her.

Once again, I pored over texts. There were as many recipes for dealing with foreign-born students as there were authors. One technique would have Mrs. Isaacs memorize words that rhymed, like *bay, day,* and *pay;* another method involved looking at pictures and learning the words to go with them. Only one method struck a chord: relate the new language to the old one and point out what the two had in common. I would try that approach with Mrs. Isaacs.

The next lesson began well. Mrs. Isaacs wrote the date, hesitating only on the number, and she even managed the word *Dear*. Then she sat back and waited for praise.

"That's terrific, Mrs. Isaacs. Now we have to add the cleaning woman's name. What is it?"

"Betty."

"Which letter do we begin with?"

Mrs. Isaacs smiled slyly. "I should tell the teacher?"

"Think now, Mrs. Isaacs. Betty. Buh. Buh."

Mrs. Isaacs looked confused for a minute, then she brightened, said "aha," and made a lowercase *f*.

"No, Mrs. Isaacs, not an *f*, buh."

"Don't buh me. Tell me what to do."

"You make a *b*, Mrs. Isaacs. Think of Yiddish. Think of Hebrew. This is like *bais* in Yiddish, *beth* in Hebrew."

Mrs. Isaacs burst into tears. "Who knows from *beth*? My family was poor, and they put me to work when I was eight. I never learned *beth*."

My eyes widened in surprise. "How can that be? Jews revere schooling—"

Mrs. Isaacs shook her head. "In my family only the boys. I didn't learn then and I'm not learning now. I just remember the words you learned me."

As the tears kept coming, I patted Mrs. Isaacs on the hand and stroked her hair. I felt helpless and, more than anything else, wanted to escape the older woman's grief and shame. Maybe someone else, someone with more skill and experience, could help the dressmaker realize that letters equal sounds and *b* was less elusive than she thought.

CAROL SCHWALBERG *is a fifth-generation New Yorker who now considers herself a Californian. Her short stories, poetry, nonfiction books and newspaper and magazine articles have appeared in this country and abroad. Her favorite pastimes are travel, visiting art galleries, and spreading malicious gossip.*

One Step at a Time

Anina Robb

"I'm David. The principal told me to come to your class."

It was spring, and at the doorway of my sixth-grade classroom was a boy, shorter than most of the other sixth graders, dressed in khaki pants, a white shirt, wing-tip shoes, and little round spectacles; all the other students in my room wore jeans, T-shirts, and sneakers. In the past eight months I had learned to roll with the punches that the administration threw me, and I knew that I had no choice in accepting or turning away students. So, I stepped aside and let David step into my classroom. He sat at the front, with the center group, and filled out emergency cards, inventory cards, and assessments for the remainder of that first period. Later, in the office, I found out from the secretary that David came from self-contained special education class, and that the principal had decided to mainstream the special education students because the board of education was eventually going to mainstream them all anyway. What was mainstreaming? I had no accurate idea, but I was worried that David could possibly be a behavior problem, or that he would fall behind in the class and I would not have the skills to help him succeed. It turned out, though, that David was one of my most motivated students. He worked hard, listened, asked questions, and checked out books from the class library.

At first, I sensed that David was anxious about being in a new class. He would only talk to me about school work. He would not linger after class like many of the other students. Slowly, he warmed to me and the other students. One day, David told me that he was going to be a lawyer. Another day, he told me that his mother had died three years before and that was when he started misbehaving in school. He couldn't look at me when he whispered that his teachers had put him in a special education class and that he had been in one ever since. I did not know whether to feel anger or sorrow. After David confided in me more, the equation seemed simple: a boy of eight loses his mother to AIDS; he is not allowed to visit her at the hospital; he is not taken to the funeral; one day, his mother is just gone, and he is sent to live in a foster home until his aunt and uncle can adopt him. I thought to myself that I would have acted out in school, too. Is that a justifiable reason to put a student in special ed?

David grew into one of my most motivated students. That spring, the class read Greek myths from novels that had been donated by a friend of mine who worked at a publishing company. David marched to the library on his own and checked out a bookbag-full of books on Greece and Greek myths. He brought the books to class and asked if he could come up at lunch-time and read them. I was so impressed by his curiosity and his eagerness to learn that I gladly gave up my lunch periods to supervise him. David designed flash cards of the Greek gods: on the front, he drew a picture of the god or its symbol; on the back he wrote down all of the information he knew about the god. This was such a great idea that I asked him if we could turn it into a class activity. David grinned from ear to ear.

At the end of that year, I stepped forward and requested to keep David with my class. We would all be moving up together to the seventh grade. The principal told me that she did not like David, that she thought he was sneaky and effeminate. I simply said, *"I would like him to be in my class because he is a hard worker and I think we could learn a lot together."* The principal grimaced and added him to my roster.

The next fall, when seventh grade started, I raised the level of difficulty of the class; my students rose to the occasion. I instituted the Reading and Writing Workshop because the school had changed to block schedules. The class loved the posted agendas, the reading strategies, the read-alouds, the writing centers, and the mini-lessons. We were working like a finely tuned engine. The room was filled with charts of lessons on everything from making predictions to personification. There was no set curriculum in the school, so my seventh-grade class was following a curriculum I had developed.

At a faculty meeting in December, the principal said that because there might be an audit, she was changing the classes around. All special education students who had been "mainstreamed" last year needed to be moved back into one class with a certified special ed teacher. New class lists would be in our boxes on Monday. I was outraged that the students whom I had worked with for two years were going to be removed and reshuffled into new classes. I was determined to keep David with me. After the meeting I told the principal that I was not losing David. She said, *Yes. You. Are.*

The next day I conferred with the special education liaison who advised me that all I could do was try to get David reevaluated and decertified. That night I called David's aunt and uncle. They asked me if a principal was allowed to switch students around to different teachers without informing the parents. I said that I did not know. They told me that David really enjoyed my class. He had told them that I listen and that he likes the way that I teach. They did not want him to be shuffled around. Even though being decertified meant that David would not receive special services like guidance counseling, his aunt and uncle agreed to let me try to get him decertified as a special education student.

The next day I revealed my intentions to the principal. She scowled, shook her head, and said that I better do it quickly. So I heeded her warning, started the paperwork in process, filled out endless forms, conferred with the evaluation teams, and finally, set up a test date and interview date for David.

In the meantime, the principal reconfigured the classes. David was allowed to remain with me because his case was pending. But other students were crying in the hallways, showing their anger by throwing books and papers on the floor, by swearing and making oaths. In a way I was lucky because my class had only six new students. However, these were six students who, I worried, would fall behind. Through no fault of their own, they knew nothing about the Reading and Writing Workshop; they were not used to writing and reading independently; they were not used to my classroom order; they did not know how to keep journals or write book reviews. I could tell that they were frustrated and anxious. I wanted them to be part of the class, but who knew if classes would change again tomorrow? How much time was I supposed to spend going backward?

When the letter arrived in my mailbox that the evaluation team had agreed to decertify David as a special ed student, I was overjoyed. I felt that if I had done nothing else as a teacher, this would have been enough. David would now remain in class with me and the friends that he had made. That evening when I called his aunt and uncle to tell them the good news, his uncle started to cry and thanked me for caring about his nephew. The next day, at the end of literacy class, David handed me a piece of loose-leaf paper and zipped out of the room. He had written a letter to me which I have hung up on my desk at home. On the last line he wrote, *Ms. Robb you are my family.*

I wish that it would have been possible for me to be a voice for each and every student in my school. But teaching has taught me an important lesson: recognize your own capabilities and limitations. Teachers in gargantuan school systems have to choose their battles wisely or they risk being squashed by the system's sheer size. Change, I came to understand from my principal's belligerence and David's triumph, is sometimes best achieved in small steps. And hopefully, even though I was an activist for one child, the reverberations of that action will be felt for a long time to come.

ANINA ROBB *has taught Middle School students in Houston, New York City, and Virginia. Presently, she writes for* The Great Source *and* Scholastic *and teaches a sixth-grade reading and writing workshop at Powhatan School in Boyce, Virginia. She earned an M.F.A. in poetry from Sarah Lawrence College and an M.A. in English from Hollins College. Her poems and essays appear in both books and literary journals.*

The Advantages of Deep Water Swimming

Gwynn Gacosta

It's the last day of school, and I'm helping my partner teacher, Ms. M., dismantle her classroom. I sweep up broken crayons, torn homework sheets that were never completed, and little candy wrappers under the radiator. Ms. M. takes down her alphabet from the front of the classroom and sighs. "My first classroom," she says, looking wistfully around the half-naked room. She then puts her cutout word-wall words in a small envelope marked, "fifth grade."

This reminds me of the alphabet in my classroom. Having no money for letters to trace, let alone board paper, I'd drawn the block letters myself on construction paper found under a pile of dirty boxes. Andre, one of my kids, helped to cut and glue them to the old, paint-chipped walls. Last Friday, the kids had taken down the faded letters and word wall, and asked me where to put them. "Just throw everything in the trash," I said. Didn't think twice about it. By 3:30 I was sitting at my empty desk, staring at my empty room, feeling empty.

Andre peeked in. "Ms. Gacosta? Do you need any more help?"

"No, thank you, honey. Everything's done." I looked into his elusive brown eyes. "It's a little sad, isn't it?"

Andre half-grinned, and nodded.

"Is that why you were so quiet during our last reading class?"

Andre nodded again. Then he turned and walked out the door. "Bye, Ms. Gacosta," his voice trailing as he flew down the stairwell.

I moved to Philadelphia in February 2000. Not completely against my will, but not my first choice, either. My husband landed a job here, so we moved from San Francisco into the unknown. While searching for "my place" in the city, I applied for a position as a literacy intern teacher with the Philadelphia School District. As a literacy intern, I would work in a primary-grade classroom with an experienced teacher, and focus specifically on reading. The training would earn me six graduate credits toward a teaching degree. I didn't necessarily want a teaching degree, but I didn't *not* want one either. I had been working with children for the past five years, dipping my foot in and out of water that *felt* perfect, but wasn't enough to get me to swim. This was an opportunity to walk further into the waves.

The district called me for an interview in March. I arrived to find at least a hundred other prospective interns, and this was one day out of two weeks of interviews. Despite this, I knew I would become one of them. At thirty, I knew what I wanted to do with my life: to work in public schools with inner-city children—children whose parents did not have access to the best schools or the best ways to make ends meet. It was my belief, as spiritual as it was political, that quality education was a right not a privilege. I believed in the potential of public school. Though I had had a positive public school experience, the kids I wanted had not. They had trouble even coming to school, seeing it as a place where it was harder for them to learn than it was for me to teach. I wanted kids who couldn't read, whose pens didn't move across the page with ease, who couldn't express themselves on paper the way they could with their fists. I *wanted* them. My goal? To share what I loved: books, reading, writing. I wanted kids to trust that a book would take them somewhere good. To be able to pick up a pen and write how much they either loved or hated what they saw around them. To show them a way to their own voices. Lofty? Maybe. But I would settle for nothing less.

In August, money for a new "Middle Years" program came and a position was offered. Ignoring all rumors of a teacher's strike and the district's bad reputation, I grabbed it. I was to work in a fifth-grade classroom, for the "transitional program." My children were children who did not pass their SAT-9s and couldn't move on to the next grade. My task was to prepare them for their second-chance tests.

Little did I know of the rough waters ahead: two inexperienced partner teachers (one after the other); a classroom with books our children couldn't read; my own classroom (piled high with dust, boxes, old desks, and outdated classroom materials); more time spent in training than in teaching; the West Philly neighborhood that would become famous for the biggest drug massacre in Philadelphia history; and more information about myself than I ever knew existed.

My working relationship with my first partner teacher, Mr. K., was disastrous from the start, precipitated by the fact that he did not prepare, and held two other jobs. He was a "screamer"—did not believe that speaking to children in a calm, respectful tone would get the same desired response as did shouting and kicking desks. He yelled out of frustration, and out of a reluctance to accept his present situation: a classroom of African American students who had academic and/or discipline problems, who read two grades below grade level, and spent fourth grade with a long-term sub. Not to mention having to supervise an intern with a master's degree, a different teaching philosophy, and more experience with inner-city kids than he had.

Our relationship exploded one day during lunch detention. Some kids were reading books around me while I was eating lunch. Mr. K. barked at them to put the books away and asked to speak to me outside the classroom.

"They circle around you because you're so soft, they get away with anything," he said, finger in my face. "They're in detention, this is not fun and games."

"Maybe you should make that clear to them instead of yelling at me."

"You need to learn not to take everything so personally."

"If you spoke to me as an adult, maybe I wouldn't take your tirades so personally."

"As far as I'm concerned, if I end up losing you as an intern, it would be fine by me, because I need someone in there who's on the same page as I am."

"I'd be happy to talk to the principal with you."

He shot me this look of superiority. "You know, I could break down everything you've done wrong in the classroom," he said.

Fed up, I responded, "I'm so sick of your shit."

This was October, and I thought, "He has to go." The principal, in an effort to make the best of the situation, assigned me six of the lowest-skilled readers and six of the lowest-skilled students in math, and put me in my own classroom in the mornings. This on top of the four students that I had to prepare for their tests. This meant that I had to learn how to make lesson plans, choose appropriate material, assess, and assure these kids that I knew what I was talking about.

By the end of December, Mr. K. was gone. One of our students accused him of pushing and threatening him in the coat closet, while the rest of the class watched through the window. Mr. K. then conspired to get the kids to say that he didn't touch him. Because he had been written up for not having a grade book or lesson plans, this was the final straw.

The irony is that because of him, I had to jump into the water. Left with my own group, I had to decide: do I float through the year, or do I kick? I *had* to teach, and this made me angry. Angry because Mr. K. couldn't teach me how to teach and I couldn't fall back on his experience. All this time I had wanted what was easy: to observe, be supportive, play second fiddle. Instead, I was left alone, hoping for a substitute.

But no one ever came. When we came back from Christmas break, the kids were divided and sent to other classrooms to sit, do worksheets, and wait. This made them unruly and resentful, and difficult to control. My children stayed with me in the morning. They were lucky, for at least they had some stability as well as some instruction, but they were no less hard to deal with. With Mr. K.'s absence, I faced terrible days, my pity for the children washed out by pity for myself. I'd go home, angry with my husband because he couldn't tell me that I didn't have to go back there. Sometimes I would crawl under the living room table just to feel safe. I'd go to sleep, praying that daylight wouldn't come too quickly.

In February, daylight arrived in the form of Ms. M., a teacher from the suburbs who agreed to take us on. She had never had her own classroom, but she had assisted classrooms for years, just like I had. She came with her own supplies and ideas, but above all, she came with the desire to teach and the hope that she would make a difference. However, she had little understanding of the socio-economic circumstances of the children in our classroom. Mutual understanding between Ms. M. and her students would not come easily, and I became a cultural bridge—my Filipino self, trying to help this Italian-Polish teacher relate to African American kids! Still, I welcomed it—with glee—over yelling and lack of direction.

Difficult days passed, from February through June, teaching in my own classroom in the morning, helping her in the afternoon, tutoring before and after school. But I loved my kids, and together, I learned to teach and they learned to appreciate books. Last Friday finally arrived, and I was sitting at my empty desk, staring at my empty walls. Marveling at how fast it had all gone by, and my, oh my, how much I'd grown.

I am straightening out Ms. M.'s classroom library, my mind on the year's accomplishments. All of my students jumped one or two reading levels, one of them moving from first-grade level to fourth. The group of four passed their second-chance tests. All of my students like to read now, and that makes me smile most of all.

I learned that preparation meant confidence. I would prepare during the week for the following week and started coming in early and staying late. Sometimes, during my journaling, I would jot down teaching ideas, occasionally falling asleep while teaching in my head. Still I managed to save time for myself.

I had to fight for instructional time against the millions of distractions that took away from what was important. I learned to choose which diversions were worth the battle for the students' attention once the diversions came to an end.

I would explain everything as clearly and as slowly as possible, knowing that I would probably explain it all over again. And again.

I would spend a long time on one good thing and explore the countless ways to look at it.

I learned that neither the smartest nor the most troubled student can ever lead the class as well as a good teacher. I learned to set rules that promoted respect, remembering that tomorrow brings not only change but also second chances.

I learned to take care of discipline challenges through detailed written accounts, and constant, if annoying, communication with parents. Similarly, I learned to handle children with learning issues twice as fast, and to do the paperwork necessary to fight for the help they needed.

After this year, I feel like I've found my destiny, for even the worst parts of this experience made me a better person. Now, whether I teach in a classroom or in a program of my own, it will be in a community such as the one in West Philly, full of children I want to work with, where the water is deep and overwhelming, but once you dive in, it's even more refreshing and rewarding than you could've ever imagined—much more than if you'd just dipped your toes in.

Andre's therapeutic support worker, Mr. D., called me a couple weeks ago, to let me know how Andre was doing.

"We were in the library, reading, and he came to a word he didn't know. So he started to sound out the word, letter by letter 'til he figured it out."

"Fabulous!" I said. Moving him from kindergarten reading level to first-grade, then to second-grade, had been like pushing against a boulder.

"I know. So all the things you kept pounding into him about paying attention to the letters in front of him, he really did learn it. He wasn't just going through the motions to get us off his back!"

I laughed, thinking of all the times when Andre had refused to do anything for me, out of frustration. He continued, "I told him, 'If Ms. Gacosta were here, she'd be real proud of you.' And he had that big ol' Andre grin on his face."

I thanked Mr. D. and hung up. Then I thought about all of my kids and what we'd overcome this year, together. Perhaps

my greatest accomplishment is that they may not need me anymore.

GWYNN GACOSTA *is a 2000 graduate of San Francisco State
University's Creative Writing graduate program and has worked as a tutor, mentor, teacher's assistant, and intern in San Francisco, Oakland,
and Philadelphia public schools. She would like to use her experience
to start her own after-school program, incorporating reading, creative
writing, and other artistic activities.*

From the Mouths of Students

Mark Sutton

When I was in third grade, I wrote "Mr. Sutton, Kindergarten Teacher" on a piece of wood that I used for playing school. The age I wanted to teach changed as I aged, but that desire did not. All the teachers I admired growing up seemed to work effortlessly. My mother, who has taught piano since she was sixteen, displayed intense patience working on a piece of music, repeatedly, with a crying kid. Mildred Suits, yearbook advisor at North Lenoir High School, pushed her yearbook staffers, including me, to consistently produce award-winning books. Author and University of North Carolina at Chapel Hill professor Doris Betts' sharp and specific feedback, while respecting the student-writer's effort and visions, improved many a story in her fiction workshops. My chance to follow their example came during my second year of graduate school at the University of South Carolina at Columbia. As part of my assistantship, I was assigned to teach composition. Preparing for the class filled up my summer. It even invaded my dreams.

Imagination has always been a personal strength, but these dreams went way beyond my usual fantasies. The entire theoretical and historical knowledge of composition and rhetoric resided in my mind, accessible at super-computer speed. Class discussions ran effortlessly as I responded to my students' questions and comments with exactly the right phrase, providing the nurturance they needed to mature as writers and scholars. They took copious notes and read every assignment carefully. While they weren't all great writers, they tried hard and improved with my help. All my students loved smart, kind, and professional Mr. Sutton.

I really hoped this dream would come true. My tendency to fixate on the worst-case scenario, however, was nearly as potent a part of my personality as my imagination and reminded me of two things. First, I knew little about teaching college-level writing. I was, at that point, a literature major. An undergraduate course on teaching writing had shown me how to work with students in lower grades. I hoped most of the information would be transferable, but I was sure it wouldn't be that simple. Second, public speaking terrifies me, especially if I don't have a script to read. Teachers in small classes have to adapt every second. With its usual charm, the doomsayer part of me decided Mark—the bumbling, idiotic fool whose only redeeming feature was a well-meaning, if stupid, heart—would do most of the teaching. Mr. Sutton would rarely make an appearance.

The first few weeks of class seemed to reflect the nightmare. Dr. Carolyn Matalene, who taught the training course for new instructors, guided me and my fellow newbies through the opening decisions, but my paranoia wanted the whole semester set up immediately, eliminating the need for last-minute decisions I would most certainly screw up. While most of the students tried to do what I asked, they apparently disliked the assignments I developed on my own. Many of their reactions came, I suppose, from the hour. We met from 3:35 to 4:25 on Mondays, Wednesdays, and Fridays; by then, everyone needed a lot of caffeine to function. Most of the trouble, though, was caused by my lack of poise. I stumbled through class discussions, unable to answer the simplest question with a coherent sentence. For those weeks, Mr. Sutton was less impressive during the day than at night. Mark acted like I had imagined he would.

Dr. Matalene assigned *The St. Martin's Guide to Teaching Writing* to us new teachers. While reading the section about end-of-course evaluations, a brainstorm struck. Why wait? Mid-course evaluations could help me salvage the class and repay my students for the crap I had put them through. This act may seem like masochism (a common pastime for doomsayers), but I hoped it could ease my nerves. I tend to see only the worst; I might be misinterpreting the class. Things might have been going fine. However, I didn't expect to be that wrong.

I handled the mid-semester evaluations just like the required ones I would distribute in two months. Removing the manila envelope from my backpack, I told the class I wanted their feedback about the class. They needed to give me specific suggestions. "You suck," no matter how accurate, wouldn't help me improve the class. After enlisting a volunteer to take the surveys to my mailbox, I headed for my office, nausea squishing my guts.

The wait made me long for the usual boredom associated with my office hours. All I could think about was their responses. My students were sharp, and they probably remembered everything I had done wrong since the first day. Once my watch read 4:35, I slid the envelope out of my mailbox (at arms length, as if it were a furious skunk) and slunk into the department lounge. I figured I could at least be comfortable while learning about my shortcomings.

I skimmed the first set of questions, those on the course design. Few students liked the reading quizzes. They felt I gave them too infrequently and made the questions either too hard or too easy, never average. I agreed; the questions were hard to write, and anyway I preferred to spend class time working with students on writing instead of checking their reading comprehension. I could drop the quizzes and add other graded assignments. The students also wanted more time between the rough draft of their essays and the final, including an additional peer review session. Again, I could understand and implement their request. I like plenty of time to revise myself. The schedule was too tight to move the last essay, but I could jiggle the due dates for the others. Hey, I thought, these aren't so bad. We all want the class to work the same way.

We didn't agree on everything, however. The students wanted to read more literature. The next course, writing about literature, would satisfy this need, and I felt they needed more practice with general, functional writing. Then, they asked for more discussions of grammar, which made me wonder if I wasn't boring them enough. Based on their papers, each student seemed to have his or her own problems with grammar. If I lectured on those grammatical issues one student needed to learn, I'd take time away from everyone. We could talk about the common infractions, but I preferred to work with them one-to-one on specific issues.

So far, all the comments had been either things I could and would change, or things I couldn't change for reasons my students should accept. I went back through the sheets, looking at the questions about my teaching style. That area, in my opinion, needed the most work. My doomsayer part pointed out everything I did wrong: mumbling instructions, looking everywhere but at the students, not answering questions accurately. I prayed my students would offer some suggestions beyond "find another job."

When I wrote this essay, I couldn't find the midterm evaluations in my records. Still, I remember some of the responses:

"You seem really nervous. Relax."

"You might want to cut down on the Diet Cokes."

"Calm down. You've done fine so far."

"You're so nervous you're making me nervous!"

I expected irritation. I expected suppressed rage. I expected even a few outright insults. I did not expect support and praise. I expected they would not have realized how close I was to a heart attack until I dropped dead in class, lesson plans permanently clutched in my left hand. They were usually nice to me, but I thought most of that came from good manners. Their words made me think they not only liked me but thought I wasn't doing that bad a job.

The following Monday, my class and I talked about the evaluations. I agreed to stop giving quizzes; the students still kept up with the assignments, writing more detailed journal responses. I agreed to work more time into the schedule for peer review. I gave my reasons for not teaching literature. I explained why my method of teaching grammar, marking selected sections of their papers, would be more useful and engaging than lectures on comma splices. We did, briefly, talk about verb tense that day. Lastly, I thanked them for their concern about my nerves and said I would try to relax.

I don't think I ever really did with that group. Teaching was still too new, even with a great group willing to work with me through my first semester. I loosened up more later, with other classes, and with more experience and study in my head. While I've enjoyed working with most of my students, that first group holds a special place in my memory. They liked Mr. Sutton, but they thought Mark taught just as well.

I would like to thank the Columbia II chapter of the South Carolina Writer's Workshop for offering suggestions to an earlier version of this essay.

MARK SUTTON *is a fourth-year Ph.D. student in composition and rhetoric at the University of South Carolina at Columbia. He is currently serving as assistant director of the Writing Studio, a supplemental instruction program for students in first-year composition.*

Theme for English 9

Carolyn Alessio

The announcement came over the intercom before the school's first dance of the year: "No mini-skirts, no spaghetti straps, no gang colors."

"What's left?" asked one of my despairing students. It seemed a natural question at the high school where I had just begun teaching, located a half block from a crack house, and not far from the dividing lines between territories for rival gangs. Drive-by shootings were not uncommon, though my students were savvy in a way that made me realize the gaps in my own survival skills. When gunfire erupted, the students knew to roll toward the curb as a mundane fact of life, just as I knew to avoid northbound Lake Shore Drive when the Cubs were playing, four blocks from my condo.

When I took my first job as a high school teacher, on Chicago's struggling West Side, I had few illusions about learning street smarts (I still made some laughable errors in Spanish, the predominant language of the neighborhood). I did not fancy myself one of those neophyte teachers in movies who come to the ghetto karate-kicking and inspiring their tough-but-tender-hearted students. I did, however, have some hope of connecting with my students through literature. Stories and poems provided an arena where writers could be daring and reflective, and I hoped to inspire my students to do the same. But in all my lesson plans and methods learned from pedagogy courses, I forgot to allow for the unique perspectives my students would bring to the work.

The school where I teach is an uncommon one; in an area of overcrowded and violence-ridden public high schools, ours is a private, Jesuit school dedicated to preparing Mexican and Mexican American students for college. The poverty level of the students' families is approximately 80 percent, so the school operates according to a pioneer method: students work one day a week at local offices to pay for their own tuition. Admission is competitive, and the students are bright and resilient. As a result of the school's unusual setup, the students experience a wide variety of environments. Their knowledge is both fascinating and challenging.

During my third week of class, I introduced the students to a poem by Stephen Dunn, "Biography in the First Person." A colleague had designed a writing exercise around the poem and I was eager to try it. The poem is a clever look at different versions of Dunn's own life, and I thought the students might enjoy the blend of invention and truth.

Erica, a student who painted her fingernails with liquid paper, began to read the poem aloud to the class. Most of the first section went fine, though I could tell that some of the students' minds were wandering. It was past 3 P.M., a half hour from dismissal, and from the large windows came the calls of paleterías or ice cream vendors, and the shouts of young children released earlier from elementary school.

"This is not the way I am. / Really, I am much taller in person," Erica read, her voice rarely committing to emphasis. I continued to listen and wonder if I should have picked a poem that spoke more to my students—Dunn was White, and probably close to sixty by now. I had always enjoyed his work, but could see how it might not grab my students as, say, a story by Sandra Cisneros, whose work I had planned for later in the semester.

Then Erica reached a memory section of the poem, and the line, "My father a crack salesman." Suddenly everyone sat up and began nudging each other. Voices emerged from the sleepy, late-day haze, and Erica paused.

"That's sad," said Ali, an ardent fan of Winnie the Pooh.

"His father, yeah," said Luis, who rarely spoke.

"What?" I said, sounding like a teenager just accused of something, but I was genuinely confused.

"The crack dealer, his dad," called out a student.

I looked down at the mimeograph of the poem. "Oh," I said, "crack salesman?"

The students nodded their heads at me.

"Remember when we talked about vernacular?" I said; "You know; lingo?" but the students were breaking off into small conversation groups as I tried to speak over them. "'Crack' meant 'great' in the '40s and '50s," I tried again, guessing at the era; "it meant crackerjack—excellent."

The students blinked at me. "He can write about his dad," said one young man. "It's not like he did crack himself."

I tried to imagine Stephen Dunn, who in my memory was bearded and wore tweed (this may have been a conjuring), smoking in the alley behind the nearby crack house, wearing a sweatshirt with a hood. Months later, when he would be announced as winner of the Pulitzer Prize, it was hard for me to watch him on television without thinking of this image.

"But crack wasn't invented in the '40s and '50s," I told the students. "It's an '80s drug, I think."

The students sighed. Erica flicked her liquid-paper-covered nails against her desk.

"I'd tell you if that was what he meant," I said. "But I don't think so."

"Ms. Alessio," said Miguel, who sat near the front, "you don't have to clean up the poem for us."

For the next few weeks I began to comb the texts for possible double-entendres or misunderstandings. When I recounted the "crack" incident to friends, one pointed out that nobody would say crack "salesman," but "dealer." "What would you say these days? Fine purveyors of crack?" mused a friend, Keith, who also was a teacher.

I didn't want my students to give up on poetry, or to think that I was sanitizing verse for them, so I searched for work that would speak more to the students, and with less ambiguity.

Since the parents of most of my students worked in factories (and some of my students had, too), I brought in Philip Levine's "You Can Have it." The poem is a bittersweet reflection on 1948, the year the poet was twenty, when he worked in a Detroit soda-bottling factory, crating products headed for "the children of Kentucky." Levine leaves few details out about the rigor of working a night shift, wearing clothes "crusted with dirt / and sweat." From my students' first-hand knowledge of factory work, I thought they would have a sense of what Levine was talking about. Before handing out the poem, I scanned it several times for modern-day lingo problems, but found none.

We read the poem aloud in class. For the first few stanzas, the students remained moderately alert. The poem takes a turn then, and begins to decry the seeming meaninglessness of factory jobs and the ways in which they blot out people's dreams.

Mindy, a soccer star, was reading: "...hands / yellowed and cracked, a mouth that gasps / for breath and asks, 'Am I gonna make it?'" I looked around and saw the other students staring down at their desks or gazing toward the window.

After Mindy finished reading, the discussion went flat. At first I tried some obvious content-based questions, in case the poem had been more difficult than I had thought, but the students readily knew the answers. They responded in lackluster voices, though, slouched in their chairs.

It wasn't until that night, as I left the school, that I fully realized my error. As I drove from the neighborhood of boarded-up buildings and signs reading "Sleeping Rooms—$35," past the lumberyard where workers were striking, I remembered Levine's words. I had been admiring his realistic details and true knowledge of the working class, when my students responded to the other half of Levine's message, the yearning and rage he feels years later, as he looks back upon a time so difficult that "that year has fallen off all the old newspapers."

I drove under a crumbling viaduct and turned onto the highway. My students knew that their parents might never have the chance to look back on such jobs, and they, themselves, might not either. When I chose the poem, I saw it as a bridge—to understanding, to perspective—and missed the indictment. I still was teaching more with myself in mind than my students. As I drove along Lake Shore

Drive that night, I couldn't shake the final line of James Joyce's "Araby": "Gazing up into the darkness, I saw myself as a creature driven and derided by vanity; and my eyes burned with anguish and anger."

Months later, when my classes read Langston Hughes' "Theme for English B," the students finally claimed poetry as their own. We were preparing to read Lorraine Hansberry's "A Raisin in the Sun" and I added a few of Hughes' poems as a segue. The students responded to "Harlem (A Dream Deferred)" with some diffidence, but the afternoon we read "Theme for English B," the atmosphere of the classroom transformed. Alex, a student who sat near the back, volunteered to read aloud Hughes' description of his daily journey from a college classroom filled with White students and instructor, to his room in a Harlem Y.

The poem was rather long—forty lines—but none of the students fidgeted as Alex continued, then ended with Hughes' final message to his writing instructor: "As I learn from you, / I guess you learn from me— / although you're older—and white— / and somewhat more free. / This is my page for English B."

Before I could generate a discussion, the students clamored to write their own poems. It was near the end of the period (and the day), but they were so enthusiastic that I quickly fashioned an assignment: Write about a transition in your own life—school to home; school to work; work to home. Show us your journey and yourself, rather than us tell about it.

For the first time, that afternoon the students remained a little after the bell, adding to their drafts, reading a few lines aloud to each other. As I moved between desks, I saw titles, pictures, scratched-out lines. Voices and pens worked together, and I silently praised Langston Hughes.

The next day the students produced their poems. Many students had worked through lunch and their study hall to finish them in the computer lab. A colleague, who was supervising the computer lab, told me she was amazed by the poems she saw on the screens.

"Her long painted nail touched the / Down button on the elevator," began a poem by David, who worked one day a week in a law firm. For many of the students, the transition from downtown corporations to home provided endless material for these poems. David's poem, "Me Here, Me There," showed the competing images David encountered downtown: White Lexuses with tinted windows; homeless men who ranged in appearance from "White and pale" to "pitch-Black and dry like the deserts of Mexico."

David described how he did not feel truly comfortable until he and his classmates were on the bus, headed back toward their own neighborhood: "Alex can once again throw apples out the window, / Lily can yell at everyone, and tell them to shut up."

For other students, the poem provided an opportunity to critique school and teachers. Yesenia, one of my most conscientious students, chided me for a banal refrain: "We need more of the / Show and do not tell details; / Here and there and / Similes and metaphores (sic) everywhere!"

Listening to and reading the poems, I felt like I was being offered an opportunity to accompany my students on journeys, not as a confidante but more as a bus passenger seated a row or two behind them. It was closer than I ever had been before with my class, and I was eager to accept any sort of proximity. Though I knew that I would make many more errors as a teacher, I felt at last that I was being offered direction from a source that surrounded me every day.

Crystal, a fierce athlete who rarely showed enthusiasm in class, gave me her poem on time that day. Entitled "Theme for English 9," her poem articulated the mixed emotions she felt when riding back home from her weekly job downtown: "I see the streets / Some bright and clean / But some are dirty, / not neat. / The gangs outside / always looking for trouble / or just waiting for someone / to step up to."

CAROLYN ALESSIO'S *work has appeared in the* Chicago Tribune, Tri-Quarterly, Boulevard, *and elsewhere. She is the editor of the forthcoming, bilingual anthology,* Las Voces de la Esperanza / The Voices of Hope.

Dollars and Points

Marcus Goodyear

The man continued to berate me for an hour and a half on Thursday after school. I was worthless, useless, mean, deceptive, vindictive, unfair, evil, disgusting, power-hungry, bitter, manipulative. At one point he unbuttoned his shirt to show me the scar from his throat surgery.

"Sir, you don't have to prove you had surgery. I believe you."

His daughter, my student, was there. His wife was there. My department head and principal, too.

Every time I began a defense, every time I tried to explain plagiarism, he interrupted and insulted me. My department head tried to defend me. My principal tried to defend me. I quietly put away the letter that explained why my student was a wonderful person and why she still would not make a passing grade on her plagiarized research paper. It was a statement of my belief system, my values, my faith in God, my hope in teachers and students, my disappointment in the student's actions, and my confidence that she would accept the consequences and learn from her mistake.

I had forgotten about her parents.

No matter what I began to say they interrupted. I just couldn't make them understand that I valued their daughter and loved her as my student—even though she would fail the six weeks for plagiarizing her final research paper.

Of course, it all worked out in the end. A year later I would read her name at graduation with a strange sense of pride. But I didn't know that when I was listening to this man telling me how evil I was.

"I can't believe you think this is a just punishment," he said. "This isn't just. It's a power trip. I've seen young teachers like you before. Look at you just sitting there with your smug little new teacher self, enjoying the power you have over me and my family. We hate teachers like you. You disgust us. This decision disgusts us."

I didn't know what to say. How can any teacher respond to such a statement?

My department head spoke up, "I think you don't know Mr. Goodyear very well. I know that he puts everything he has into this job. He dedicates himself to these students."

There was a brief silence in my room. We were all sitting in a circle of student desks. I had tried to let us begin as equals. I had hoped to raise the discussion to issues of morality and ethics. I had assumed that this family cared about more than just eligibility. But they did not. Why should they? So many things in our school and society point toward the bottom line. We grade product, not process. We are valued by our paychecks, not our contributions to humanity. If teachers don't get paid much, they must not be very important. If a writer's books don't sell, then he must not be very good. If a movie doesn't make millions of dollars, it isn't a success. Why would I expect a student to care about abstractions like quality and morality?

Eventually, I realized that the conference would never end until I ended it.

"I don't think we really have anything else to talk about," I said. It was that simple. I believed plagiarism was wrong. They believed plagiarism was an acceptable mistake. I had already told them about most university policies against academic dishonesty: "They kick you out of college for doing this," I said. I had already explained the legal ramifications of professional plagiarism: "An author could sue you for doing this if you tried to publish." His daughter, on the other hand, would merely receive a failing grade for the plagiarized assignment. No expulsion. No lawsuit. She would just fail the assignment and consequently the six-weeks grading period. Her ineligibility was unfortunate, but unpreventable. She had cheated. It seemed so straightforward to me.

71

But their response was always the same. "Jesus Christ! Could you make this any more melodramatic? All she did was quote a paper from the Internet without using quotation marks. Nobody is going to sue her. Nobody is going to kick her out of college. She is only sixteen years old. She didn't understand."

Nor did they. Nor would they—ever. I had assumed that I could teach anyone. I taught 150 students every year. We learned about racial prejudice and sexism and deism and transcendentalism. My students were open to these abstract ideas. They wanted to learn. This man and his family didn't want to learn anything. They just wanted their daughter to compete.

I held on for a few days. But the man kept calling. Leaving voice mails for me that were more controlled.

"I know you'll do the right thing. Jesus forgave others for their sins. I know you can too."

The messages made me so angry I would assign silent reading and fume in the corner. The man was such a hypocrite.

But was I a hypocrite too? I had thought my decision through. It seemed logical enough. The student received a 50 for plagiarizing approximately half of her paper. The resulting grade for the six weeks was a 69. The number was a slap in the face, and I had arrogantly left it there as a sign of her sin. This would teach her, I thought.

It was a mistake. It was vindictive. It was mean. After only four years I was becoming as bitter as the old prunes who taught around me. "Kids just keep getting worse and worse," they would say. "This whole country is going to hell."

I could have given the girl a 0 for her paper. Her grade would have fallen nearly twenty points to a 55. No argument there. Surely her parents would not have come in to beg for fifteen points. Surely.

Then again, maybe my biggest mistake was not allowing the student to rewrite the paper. I have always been afraid of confrontations. I never mentioned the plagiarism to the student until I handed back the failing paper. She never said a word until she saw her final grade for the six weeks. She would be ineligible. When she realized this, she came to my room in tears.

It was the last day of finals before Christmas. I played the part of Scrooge.

"Is there anything I can do?" she asked.

"You plagiarized your research paper," I said.

"Is there anything I can do to fix my grade?"

There was that obsession with points again. It bugged me the way everyone views the world in terms of economics. When would anything have value on its own merit? Why did we insist on measuring in grades and dollars? I was angry and frustrated, and I took the advice of the old prunes. Let the students go to hell if they want to, but hold your ground. Don't let them lower your expectations. Once they cheat, they lose all credibility. Once they plagiarize, they forfeit their chance for a grade.

"This is serious stuff," I told her. "You plagiarized the biggest writing assignment of the year."

"I'm sorry," she said.

"Sometimes being sorry isn't enough. Sometimes there are consequences for your actions." My words came down like an ax on the conversation. I had made my decision. Have a Merry Christmas.

In some ways, I had deserved January's berating. In some ways I deserved the continuous voice-mail messages.

After almost a week, I asked my principal for advice. What would he do? I asked my department head. Miraculously neither of them had ever become cynical, and so I trusted them. "Give her the point," they said. "It isn't worth it to hold the line. They'll drag you to the school board. They'll make you look like the villain. They'll examine every minor grade under a microscope. Just give her the point and let her have a seventy."

On the grade change form I checked "teacher error." The student became eligible. She went on to the state competition that year. "What will you say to the people you beat?" I wanted to ask her. "What will you say to the students who had enough honor not to plagiarize their research papers?" But I swallowed my pride. I swallowed some of my moral self-righteousness. I even swallowed my anger at parents who will bully their way through teachers and administrators and anyone else standing between them and their

entitlements. Because I hadn't known about her dad's health problems. If the girl had just told me that she thought her father might
die, I would have given her extra time on the paper. I would have
allowed more makeup work. I would have helped her. I should
have helped her.

Part of me still felt like I was compromising academics for ath-
letics. Part of me wanted to punish the student for the actions of
her parents. But I learned an important lesson: Always err on the
side of the student.

Because I do make mistakes, of course. I made a big mistake
with that plagiarized paper—I assumed the worst of my student.
I should have given the girl a chance to confess and rewrite the
paper. Now I know to reward students for what they do well,
rather than punish students for what they do poorly. Some students will need to face consequences for their mistakes, but that
can never become my focus as a teacher. It would destroy me. It
would make me shrivel up into bitterness and indignation that the
students, the teachers, the whole educational system was just going to hell. Everyone makes mistakes in the classroom, even me.
That is what the classroom is for. And those mistakes will only
make me worthless and vindictive if I remain proud and absolute.
Like some one-room-schoolhouse tyrant. Or like the cynics down
the hall.

During that conference I also realized that no amount of points
brings value to a student's education. Passing my class, passing the
state achievement test, even passing the Advanced Placement test
were all based on an economic view of the world. These things
reduce human actions and feelings to a few numbers—either test
scores or the price of a college class. These things work as external
rewards, but the biggest rewards are always internal. In addition
to points, I can give my students respect and trust and confidence
and faith. They need to become adults; they need me to treat them
like adults.

Why would I treat them any other way?

Above all I finally realized that I teach for the students. Not
their parents. Not my peers. Not even for myself or the paycheck

at the end of every month. I teach for my students to rise above their mistakes.

And the mistakes of their teachers.

Some of them will. I know it.

MARCUS GOODYEAR *is a writer and teacher in San Antonio, Texas. He is also a loving husband and proud father.*

Going to the Library

Dee Birch Cameron

My critic teacher told me to spend the final weeks of student teaching in the school library. I need not return to his classroom, he said. I had already done well enough to earn a stellar recommendation.

But this was no triumph. The college senior and the short, middle-aged man who faced each other that morning in 1964 both looked pale and startled. Eventually he handed me the paper and pen he was holding. I signed my name. Then I gathered my notebooks and climbed the marble stairs to the second floor of Schenley High School to retreat among the books.

The teacher, Mr. Segal, was experienced in dealing with youthful failure and had developed a flair. The English department at Schenley insisted that any assignment containing a run-on sentence failed completely, and Mr. Segal would print "ROS" at the top of these papers and add "E," the failing grade. "I got a ROSE!" a student would groan, laughing through the pain. Nevertheless this sensitive, funny veteran was utterly unprepared for a student teacher who delivered her own bouquet.

The student-teaching semester at Pitt immersed us in our chosen profession. Mornings we reported to our schools to observe and practice. Late in the afternoons we attended seminars where we were encouraged to reflect on our experiences in the light of the social history of education and of current pedagogical practice.

Eventually we would be judged by an evaluation instrument, a list of questions our critic teacher would answer about us in our presence. According to Mr. Segal, my performance presaged a bright career. "You want to be the best," he told me. "And you will be. You can't be the best right now, because you're just starting out. But you will be." He ticked off the questions. I couldn't have gotten higher marks.

"Now I come to a question that only you can answer," he said finally. I realize now that he must have perfected this dramatic pause with a long line of student teachers. He read aloud. "'Does the student see himself growing in the profession in the future?' Do you?" He smiled with such expectancy and fondness that I could hold back neither tears nor the truth.

"No," I whispered. "I actually don't ever want to do this again." Surprised both by the question itself and the realization that he had not seen through me, I was driven to confess. Student teaching had convinced me I did not want to become a high school English teacher.

"Do you consider this an onerous task?" he asked, obviously shocked and hurt.

"Oh, no," I assured him. "I think it's a wonderful, important job. I admire people who do it. I just don't want to do it myself." I stumbled, trying to make him understand.

It seemed impossible. He was devoted and enthusiastic. He had seen in me a green but kindred spirit and been mistaken. Still, ever the educator, he pulled himself together and devised the library plan as a way for me to finish out my time.

"Teaching is always hard at first," he said gently, as I prepared to leave. It was early in the morning, and students milled outside waiting for the first bell. "And your new husband's just gone off to the Army. You may change your mind. Don't close the door on it completely," he said, as I let myself out of his classroom. In those final few weeks, we nodded wordlessly as we passed in the crowded halls.

I remember the sighs of disgust when Mr. Segal first introduced me to his senior English classes that September. "Man, I waited three years to get you," a boy complained, "and now this!" He gestured in my direction. Only four years older than my students, I was still tender from my own high school rejections and realized I had returned to a milieu in which I had never been very happy the first time.

As I listened to the fervor of my fellow student teachers, I understood that people taught for better reasons than a conviction that it was all an English major could do. There were people my own age, no better at teaching than I, who nevertheless felt entitled to stand in for stars like Mr. Segal. They welcomed their futures, while I felt like a beef cow navigating the ever narrowing shoot at the slaughterhouse. I was not among the called.

Remembering my own high school days, I sympathized with the students. I resolved not to make them suffer for my mistaken career choice. Noticing that they fidgeted, I planned lessons in which no activity lasted longer than ten minutes. If the transition involved standing up and moving the chairs into new arrangements, so much the better.

When I gauged the littleness of their vocabularies, I wrote paraphrases of Shakespeare, which I passed off as the work of "a contemporary writer." I was pleased when they said the anonymous writer was easier to understand but that Shakespeare sounded a lot better. To help them memorize the sonnet form, I made strips of colored paper for them to arrange in order.

I came to hate the format that passed for class discussion, in which a teacher asked questions and all student responses were directed back through the teacher. I gave the students questions to mull over in small groups and report on. Then I asked them to read and think about issues and to talk these topics over in front of the class so that we all could see what it looks and feels like when real people discuss ideas.

"What's Going On in Vietnam?" was the topic I assigned to some of the ablest of the students. The situation had not yet worked itself into a war, and the name of the country was new to most of us. "It worked!" Mr. Segal marveled at the end of that period. "I planned to go sit in the hall and read my magazine, but I couldn't tear myself away."

Despite the occasional success, I dreaded each day. I might have been a snake charmer among cobras. I emoted and dramatized to hold their attention. On the day the university supervisor sat watching me from the back of the room, my heavy hair tumbled out of its French knot and slid to my waist, showering hairpins. I did not break character.

As a student, I had lived for English classes. Now whatever I taught seemed irrelevant and stale. No sparks flew. While the university supervisor took notes on my performance, some of the slats of colored paper in my rainbow sonnet chart slipped out of place and shuffled to the floor, as if inspired by my wild hair. I carried on.

Walking home at the end of the day, I stopped at a beauty salon and told the hairdresser to chop mine to shoulder length. My husband, who liked it, had left that morning for Fort Benning. Were he to see it again, his tolerance for loss would have been expanded by his dreadful war experiences, I rationalized.

Occasionally, when he had been slated to teach and I expected to observe him, Mr. Segal would wince as I entered his classroom. "My head aches," he would sigh.

"Let me teach then," I would invariably urge, over his protests. Eventually he would give in. I wonder now whether he knew that my lessons were prepared like choreography and hoped to convince me that I could improvise.

Once, knowing that I was discouraged because the students did not seem to remember what I taught in class, he whispered, "Teach the test." I looked astonished. Wasn't there something dishonest about that? "It's all right," he said. "You made a good test for tomorrow. Teach it all period today." I did as I was told, and the next day as they were huddled over their chair arms with pencils and paper, only one student looked up at me as if to say that he recognized the questions.

After the awful morning on which Mr. Segal filled out my evaluation form, word must have gotten around. The professors and university supervisors seemed to look at me questioningly sometimes, but I kept quiet, determined to pass as a prospective teacher until the diploma and certificate were in my hand.

The final exam in the student teaching seminar asked us to evaluate the semester's experience as it might relate to our future careers. I wrote my last college bluebook with the lyric abandon

I had not felt since composing essays in my beloved high school English classes. I was decorative, but I was honest. I laid the booklet on the instructor's desk while all around me, the true-believing student teachers wrote earnestly about lives that would diverge sharply from mine.

Most of the winter light was gone by five o'clock. The stone path leading from the building called The Cathedral of Learning down to Fifth Avenue was dark and long. Where it ended, Pittsburgh rush-hour traffic roared. Despite the ominous surroundings, I felt free.

I heard running footsteps behind me and turned to see the instructor. He waved my bluebook in his hand. "What will you do then?" he asked, breathlessly, when he caught up.

"I don't know," I admitted. "Just not this." He praised and complimented me. He wished me luck and shook my hand. "Do you know what you'll do?" he asked again. He had followed me to find out the end of the story, which was just then equally obscure to me.

As it happened, my exile to the book stacks turned into a thirty-year career in librarianship. The path to that happy conclusion was not straight and had nothing whatever to do with Mr. Segal's plan for my last few weeks of the student teaching semester. When I did find my calling, I savored all the missionary zeal and conviction of being in the right spot that I had missed while masquerading as an English teacher. In the early days of my joy, I sometimes remembered that Mr. Segal had told me to go to the library. He must have felt at a loss that winter day, almost as much as I, but he gave me better advice than either of us knew.

DEE BIRCH CAMERON *has been a public and academic reference librarian and a cataloger for a large corporation. Most recently she was a school librarian in El Paso, Texas. Her work has appeared in* The Encyclopedia of Library and Information Science *as well as many professional journals.*

Delivering the Truth

Confessions of a Teaching Fellow

John Keats

I am in my car, delivering newspapers on a Sunday morning. I have a slight headache from the sun, a wireless phone for receiving reports of a missing *Boston Sunday Globe* or *New York Times*, and, oh yes, a master's degree in English from a Jesuit university.

Despite the heat and the low-paying job, I am content. Not once this morning have I thought about the teaching I have done, or the teaching I should be doing. Parents pay over $30,000 a year to send their children to the university I attended, parents who can afford houses like the ones I am driving past in my battered '89 Pontiac Sunbird. Corinthian columns, endless brick walkways, vine-covered porches nestled in the shade of perfect trees: they all crawl past me.

This is the east side of a Boston suburb known for high taxes, low crime, comfortable living. I live on the west side, the southwest, to be exact, and I rent. I have lived here most of my life. I went through the public school system, decided on manual labor instead of heading off to college, and attended a state school eight years after graduating high school. I paid for everything myself, until good grades got me a year's worth of tuition remission in a graduate program at a distinguished university. A teaching fellowship paid for year two—and there you have it, or there I had it: proof that blue-collar effort and a work-for-what-you-want ethic could move you into elite circles. I learned from reputable scholars. I read Joyce's *Ulysses* on granite benches in a cobblestoned courtyard under a stone tower with a golden bell that struck the hours. The Jesuit priests were around here somewhere, in one of those beautiful old buildings, reading, thinking, praying. I felt connected to something important, something I would have considered, not so very long ago, out of my league. And I was teaching, teaching the sons and daughters of parents from "east sides" of comfortable towns from all over the world!

But on this Sunday morning, the bell towers and the teaching were over. I had my master's degree hanging on a wall, but my honorable money was gone, and a nagging sense of something gone wrong in my two semesters' worth of teaching freshman composition had kept me from looking for a teaching job. I had enjoyed the experience; I had enjoyed the students: so why was I here, driving around from sunrise to noon bringing people the paper they should have received? I didn't even have my own route; couldn't tell people, when they asked me what I was doing with my life, that I was a "paper boy." I wasn't. I had papers to redeliver. I was a redeliverer, rootless and lost. Why?

Grading. We used portfolios. All the teaching fellows were required to use a collected mass of materials to determine a final grade. The portfolio allowed me to avoid being completely frozen by my temporary authority as a teacher. Dare I say, as a professor? I had texts coming to my apartment addressed to Professor Keats, and a student or two, despite my admonitions, kept calling me Professor Keats. I had gone from nothing to greatness, nothing to something, so quickly. Greatness requires making great decisions—and dispensing grades is all about making great decisions.

I was terrified. But the portfolio highlighted progress and effort. Judgment wouldn't be demanded of me on the spot. It would be all right.

"Professor Keats?"

That's how he greeted me, my former student, standing in the doorway of an immense white house; the young man whose work, to me, was worthy of a D in my first semester of teaching. There was no warning. Dispatch gave me no name. They would buzz me on my high-tech walkie-talkie, squawk out an address, and I would go—in this case, to the slaughter. But there was no real warning about teaching either, despite the four-month preparation course, all the reading, all the talking. You had to do it to get it, to get the real thing, to see how you would react.

And he said it again: "Professor Keats?"

Did I know he lived in my town? Yes, he had told me early in the semester, when I had told the class where I lived. I was all about honesty. Writing teachers need to create a space where the personal is validated. Lead by example. Share. But I didn't tell them that I had never taught before. You can't reveal everything. I remember wanting to tell them, but the grading stopped me: you needed authority to give out grades. Their knowledge of my lack of teaching experience would diminish my authority; it could even inspire rebellion. As much as we all tried to act as if power and conflict weren't part of what we were doing, it was.

In class and during our weekly conferences, he was one of my most promising students. He used vivid imagery, creative forms, lively language. The only problem I could see was that everything he wrote was short, clipped. I told him that brevity was not a problem. I asked him where he wanted to go. I don't know, he said. Well, think about the image here, the Mercedes. Okay, he said. Next week, another fragment. What about the car, I said? It's hard for me to revise, he said; I can't do it. Yes, you can, I said. Time away helps; that's why drafting is so beneficial. Keep thinking. Revising is part of all good writing, I said, and revising is an essential part of this course. But he never did revise, not really.

Most of my students were uncomfortable with not receiving a grade until the end of the semester. They were used to knowing, paper by paper, where they stood in relation to the authority in the room. Despite their discomfort, most took advantage of the drafting process. The student staring at me from the doorway of his parents' home, however, the student trying to figure out what Professor Keats was doing on his front steps with a rolled-up *New York Times* in his hand, did not. We would go over a different fragment in each conference. I would direct him to the syllabus I had designed as an aid to authority. Here's the Word of the

Course, I thought. (When the Word is written, so proveth Moses, you don't have to spend time pronouncing dictums and due dates, just reminders.) He didn't believe in revision.

He believed in magic, the magic of inspiration. I did, too, a little. Wasn't it a little magical that I was here? But teaching writing is about teaching away the magic, about showing how much control you have. You must revise, I said.

I gave the students tentative grades mid-semester. His was not good. His entire portfolio consisted of sparse, hasty writing. He panicked. He e-mailed me. He came for extra conference time. He extended his drafts. The extensions were stiff. Then he stopped coming for extra help. Family problems. I warned him again. The semester ended. I read portfolios for two days. His was half as many pages as the average student's. I gave him a D and a lengthy, written explanation, mostly repetitious, of what caused the ugly grade. He picked his portfolio up from a box outside my temporary office while I was home worrying about my own grades as a graduate student.

"Hi," I finally said, handing him the newspaper. "What a surprise, huh? How's school? You're on break?"

"Yes. What are you . . . ?"

Pause. How much should I tell? How honest should I be this time? The sun seemed stronger and my headache was worse.

"I'm working part-time. Graduated—from grad school. Doing some writing, looking for a teaching job."

"Oh," he said. "Okay, well . . ."

"Well," I said. "Good to see you."

I walked to my car, staring at the rusted mess I usually never thought of beyond its ability to get me where I needed to go. Now I realized I didn't have any idea where that was. I needed time— that's what I should have told him. I'm revising my life, standing back, sizing things up, reevaluating. I started the car and the stereo blared something loud and full of guitars. I turned it down quickly, hoping he wouldn't hear and think I listened to Metallica. As a teacher, I would have promoted my knowledge of popular culture, to give the impression of being hip, in touch, cool. But I didn't want him to think I actually enjoyed heavy metal music. Professors should listen to something smarter. But it didn't matter. He had disappeared behind his parents' white door.

I felt like a fake. Meeting my nearly failed student as I am in real life—low on cash, short on musical taste, confused in ambitions—showed me what I had been trying to hide from all of my students. They were better; they were richer. I had told them to be honest, to value their experiences, to honor who they were. Small events and small memories aren't trivial, I would say; they make you. Cherish them. I, however, hid behind my teaching. I was terrified they would discover that I didn't belong under the shadow of the university's bell tower, that I didn't quite understand all of *Ulysses,* that I wasn't a professor at all.

I was a teaching fellow. I told them my title, of course, again using a facade of honesty to conceal the truth: my doubt in the ability of teaching fellows as a species. The title demands a degree of confusion, even hypocrisy, not required of a student teacher or teacher's assistant. Good teaching is a disease; literally, it should be full of dis-ease. If you're comfortable, you risk losing sight of all the issues you should be addressing. One of my best teachers in graduate school told me that after twenty-five years of teaching, he felt like an impostor every day. That gave me comfort, or, more appropriately, further discomfort. His unending analysis and evaluation of his performance made him uncomfortable and, to me, excellent at what he did. But he was a real professor. He had firm ground to stand on.

I was not real, and no matter how much I told myself that it couldn't be helped, that everyone had to start somewhere, I could not get over the dreadful possibility that my lies contributed to my students' grades (whether poor or inflated). And grades were permanent marks upon their lives, as most footprints of authority are. I wanted to tell my D student that I was sorry, that I didn't feel qualified to judge, that I hoped I hadn't held where he lived against him. I was a newspaper redeliverer, acting as if I had a route; I had been a teaching fellow, acting as if I knew how to teach. I didn't know what I was going to do in the future and, I realized, when I was teaching, I didn't know who I was. I wasn't honest with myself. That dishonesty may have cost one young man from the "east side" of town a fair grade. I don't know. But I think you should know yourself more before you stand in front of a room full of young people waiting for a professor.

Honesty has to be the base, the ground, of the teaching fellow, since the title of professor, even if it's on a package or two in your mailbox, isn't real. Doubt and torment are part of being a good teacher, but honesty is the most important part. How do you balance honesty and authority? Can you? Should I go back to campus and ask a Jesuit if faith in such balance is realistic or foolish? Maybe I will, once I get a better job.

JOHN KEATS has written an unpublished novel and several short stories. He has not yet returned to teaching, but he no longer delivers newspapers.

Counter-Inquisitive

Sean Whitson

My students think I ask *why* too often. They shift uneasily behind
their hard, Formica slabs as they lodge this complaint and then
their attention shifts back once again to the timepiece on the
wall behind me. It is as if they just wanted to get that off their
collective chests. A few of the more daring repeat that word
mockingly each time it passes through my throat and out into
the cold compartment that has, over these last five months, become our shared reality. The walls are cinder blocks. The off-
white paint that stains them was carefully selected for its subtlety;
it neither distracts the students nor allows them to drift softly
into the comfort of midday sleep. The single coat, for all of its
functionality, however, refuses to disguise the cinder blocks beneath. The rigid pattern of cement, the grid, is the only decor,
save the clock that hangs over me like a synchronized sword of
Damocles and teases them with the methodical pace of its second
hand.

They think that if Sisyphus were smart enough, he'd have bal-
anced the boulder on his hill's tiny summit. The severity of the
punishment, whether or not it fit his posthumous tardiness, is not
at issue; it is, they suppose, whatever Camus wanted it to be. Questions of justice, questions of any capitalized concept or allegorized
characteristic flirt, for them, somewhere in the ethereal fringe,
alongside transcendental philosophy and formulas for quantum
physics. It is a place they have no desire to visit, a place, they
understand, that they never need go. And as for Sisyphus' com-
pulsion, his allegiance to his perpetual task: that, too, is easily
dismissible. If he wanted to stop, they assume he would simply
have stopped.

Later in the year they will read Milton. They will read *The mind is its own place, it can make a heaven of a hell, a hell of heaven* and, by then, its poignancy will be artless and obvious. Then I will remind them of who, exactly, is proffering that observation, but that will not be until spring. That is not when we are—or where.

This is a place that prefers silence. This is a place that has only survived due to propinquity, ninety minutes to New York and half that to Philly. This is a town that will not admit that the steel business has gone and is now on the other side of the old Mason-Dixon. In this town, we teach the kids to spend their time. It was here that I was born, and to this town, from Boston, that I returned; it was here that I took a position teaching senior English, AP English, and creative writing at a Catholic—here, only a few months later, that I was quite nearly fired for the apparently anti-Catholic crime of registering as a Democrat—high school. Some mornings, on my morning commute, I don't expect the sun to rise.

They tell me that teachers, and by "they" I now mean my administrators, often feel such frustration, especially in their first year. They also told me that theirs was an especially academically advanced institution. My seniors can't write sentences, think a semicolon is a *really big comma*. My school, I found out, falsifies grades, inflates them to pass failing students and to boost their statistics. This is apparently legal and, as I found out when I complained, vehemently defended by the tuition-dependent diocese. I ask if it is moral. I am young, I am told, and think I know everything.

I suppose my idealistic quest for the comfort of objectivity was always impossible, and therefore ill-fated. I remember (as I often reminisce about past employment), driving home from a shift of meager gratuities (cursing my lot and simultaneously fortifying its worthiness), I concluded that one should wait tables at least once in one's life; I have since become a generous tipper. The unfortunate truth, and we dare not mourn for too long, is that one can never truly understand something in which one is not involved. There is inevitably a genealogy of details, and whether they are adequately extenuating is a matter for knowledgeable judgment. So, how do I debate morality with the Moralists? Who am I to defend academic integrity to an educational institution? Once again, I find myself asking.

There are still ten minutes left in the period, and the only thing keeping the students in their seats is Matthew's comic mispronunciation of Sisyphus. Even I must admit, the words sound similar. We are finished with the lesson. Camus can wait for another day, and no one is in a hurry to get to Hopkins, on the following page. As my students fold their textbooks, shove their dress-code incompliant sweatshirts into their bags, a sudden change comes over them. It is as if, without those cumbersome publications to bar it, something worthwhile might be discussed. They surprise me with the fervor of their interrogation. I am disarmed by their collective focus. In a matter of moments they have excised all of the unguarded biographical data, the stuff you don't usually give away but on which you don't really keep a close eye, but I resolved to guard my more personal responses more vigilantly. After all, I too once collected ammunition on authority figures. The principal has also made it painfully clear that there are some subjects on which I am under a strict gag order, so I am naturally wary of what I divulge.

I answered their inquiries. I was even surprised by their modesty. I told them where I went to high school (a public school a few miles away), and to college, and to graduate school. I admitted my age, my loyalty to the Red Sox, and my marital status. They were very upset about the Red Sox. I suppose I told them more than I should have, but then, I suppose, that always happens eventually. It is easy to underestimate them. The investigation is comprehensive, and when the punctual Beth, who recites along with the public address system during morning prayers and has never missed an assignment, looks up from her impeccable nails, I know I am in trouble:

Did you like Boston?
I loved it.
Why did you come back?

Matthew asserts that, if he gets out, he will never come back. And I hope he does, but I know what will be asked of him. I know that I have, albeit unhappily, contributed to the inadequacy of his preparation. And I know I am stalling, evading. I have no answer for Beth. I don't know why I am here. I am not really sure why I come in each morning, why I don't just continue to drive for indeterminate hours when I get dismissed on any afternoon. I am speechless and speech is demanded. There is only one thing I can offer to save myself from this inquisition. *What about why he left Hades in the first place?* This provokes an absence of response. *Sisyphus,* I redirect them—*he left to reprimand his wife, who when he made her choose between custom and loyalty to him, chose loyalty to him.* Beth is unimpressed. *Does that make his indenture more understandable?* She has obviously already put class behind her, as she retorts with Who cares? This time, I can tell her that I do not know.

I retreat to the shelter of my desk, as I often do, and find that the shelter is merely suggested by its ostentatious size, its histrionic refusal to adhere to the norms of the rows of inferior models. It wants to be more than a hard, Formica slab. I will retreat again, perhaps back to Boston, or the West Coast, or law school. Yet, as for tomorrow, their essays are due, and I will be passing the quizzes, graded, back. And next week. And in May.

The bell startles me, then comes the rush of relief.

SEAN WHITSON *received his M.F.A from Emerson College, and his poetry has appeared in* Plainsongs, Roanoke Review, *and other literary journals. He currently lives and works in New York City.*

Awakening

AP

My daddy was a soft man, a reader and a teacher. That's what he did, with no action in it, no hero's stories but those he read. Eyewitness accounts I sought, and from the participants themselves, not from books. My daddy couldn't give them. Instead he gave me quotes, the same kind he gave to his other kids, his students.

"Every so often," he used to tell me, "a fella gets a chance to speak his mind." He liked to proselytize: "Surface from your dim comfort, the solitude of your mind, and with clarity be heard! Seize the opportunity, such moments are rare . . . " For the most part, he noted tragically, humans pass along in a discreet flurry of politeness, missing their opportunities. He quoted Matthew Arnold:

> I knew the mass of men conceal'd
> Their thoughts, for fear that if reveal'd
> They would by other men be met
> With blank indifference, or with blame reproved;
> I knew they lived and moved
> Trick'd in disguises, alien to the rest
> Of men, and alien to themselves—and yet
> The same heart beats in every human breast!

"Most times we're left kicking ourselves," he'd smile at me, "thinking afterward of things we should have said, would have said had the circumstances been different, had we thought of it then, or had we the courage." Life at its worst, he philosophized, is an onslaught of the guilt of missed opportunity, and at its best, an exercise in forgetfulness.

In the years since his departure, my daddy's served as a character I've been unable to forget. His teachings, or more particularly the

bullet-sized phrases he used as a means for description, interpre-
tation, or analysis of everything, every concept in this world and
any other known to him, remain always near the surface of my
thoughts, like conversations ready to spring forth, whose contents
are already known, bubbling on his imagined lips if only I should
turn to them.

He rang, bothered me in the shower at six o'clock this morning.
"You missed your chance," he said.

"What chance?" I asked myself. I was thinking of this noble
idea of *impact,* of impacting other people, kids no less. That was
his mission, impacting other people's kids.

I spent a year trying to live up to him till I got selfish and started
living for myself. I was trying to escape him by walking *his* earth,
but the selfish can't escape their own guilt and pupils rarely outstrip
their teachers.

That year I spent the days as my father had for thirty-four years,
as an English teacher in a high school in rural North Carolina. It
was a last-minute thing. The market was soft. There was an offer
to string for a newspaper—ten bucks an hour. I took to teaching.
"In and out," I told myself. "I'll go to grad school next year."

As many teachers and the sons and daughters of teachers know,
this is a common illusion. Career teachers are known to commence
working under the false presumption that such teaching will be
temporary.

For me this was no false presumption. I did leave. However,
it was in the act of such leaving that my daddy tormented me
most. You see, I thought a long time about what I would say to
my students on the last day; I'd summarize the whole course and
they'd see the wisdom of it later, when they'd look back and say,
"Now that was the start of something! I was never the same after
that!"

The aim was impact, a notion my father had set out for me
but which he had never defined in words. I had watched him. His
life was what impacted, but I couldn't describe his whole life. I
couldn't tell these kids about that life because it meant too much
to me and because I knew what they would say, how some of them

would laugh and one might call out in the middle of it, "Can I go to the bathroom?" Everybody would giggle, and when it was over the girls would roll up their hair in their fingers and turn back to their sisters, and the boys would huddle up in their groups scheming and rapping, and some others who sat by themselves looking embarrassed would gaze up at the clock and wait for the bell. It would be just another story, with all the necessary pegs of drama and injections of morale. The kids wouldn't know the difference between it and the thousand others I'd told. I doubted my relevance, but worse, I doubted his.

I was more courageous at the beginning of the school year, on the first anxiety-filled day, when I didn't know any of those kids, much less cared what they thought about me. The class was World Literature, and more than once I wondered to myself, Why must the kids study old translated books? What did *Oedipus* mean to an American teen, or *Medea*, or *Cyrano de Bergerac*?

But when I thought of it seriously I remembered a thing my father liked to say: "All human stories are essentially the same. They come down to living, loving, dying. The rest is just an abstract process people build up around those things." I delivered to the kids a short lecture on the relativity of language, how it was necessary to understand not that all people are alike but how at the bottom there is commonality. There is birth, life, and death. There is a process by which we all move, and in this movement, we all participate. The art of any culture, the words spoken in many tongues, reflect the common joys and ills of our humanity. It searches, in every instance, for an underlying meaning, a substance that helps us to reaffirm the value of our own existence.

It was an optimistic speech, delivered through the blinders of youthful naïveté. I thought I would be teaching, in addition to the five-paragraph persuasive essay, "free thought." After a few weeks of teaching and the blinders gone, I noticed with dismay how working under the rumors and shadows of state tests weighed down the process of learning. I also thought, in my class the kids would forget how they were different colors and sit together, speak with one another, be real and all. But the students mixed, barring exceptions, only when I made them. Whatever divided them was, as Arnold says, deeply ordained, deeper than any college course taught me or any book I'd read described.

Aside from *Cyrano*, the curriculum centered upon some of the grimmest of human affairs. Medea murders her two children. Oedipus kills his dad and marries his mom. Ol' Reverend Kumalo struggles in vain against apartheid to rescue his prostitute sister and murderous son in *Cry, the Beloved Country*. Last was *Night*.

After reading *Night* I told them how all that stuff had really happened to Elie Wiesel—I showed them a photograph I'd gotten of him from a workshop in Greenville, just like thousands of people they'd seen before on TV from the concentration camps, all gaping at the light of the camera. After we talked over how many and where from and by what means, the inevitable question formed on their lips: "Why?" They asked me, "What made people do this?" I didn't have an answer, I only corrected the question: "What *makes* people do this?"

I told them how one of my college professors had summed up that it was mostly about ignorance, about how groups of people over time come to think some pretty odd things about themselves and those around them. Hitler's misreading of *Zarathustra* coupled with the pomposity of Wagner's music helped in part spawn the dream of a new Reich, a super society filled with "supermen."

We read the old ballad hymn from the convoluted prose of *Revolution:*

> I am the ever rejuvenating, ever creating life! Where I am not is death! I am the dream, the comfort, the hope of the oppressed! Wherever I go, new life springs from the dead rocks! I come to you to break all of the chains that crush you, to redeem you from the grip of death, and breathe young life into your veins.

For the hordes of well-wishers clapping and stomping their feet, now saluting, now placing their hands before their open mouths, these were songs of redemption shouted above the din, ironically, through the streets of Nuremberg in the rally of 1934.

The kids asked me, how could one man move so many people?

I told them it was the people themselves who moved, and not Hitler. It was the people, the mass of common men and women who made kings and presidents. Most important, what these common people did, by the thousands, became the historical "events" later credited to singular leaders.

This was an ethic I had gleaned, admittedly, from Tolstoy. But while I sputtered through my personal enlightenment my students seemed to gravitate toward a certain fatalism, a notion that as individuals they were powerless, that their fates would be decided by great leaders like Hitler, Roosevelt, or Martin Luther King, so that finally in my quest to teach free thought I began to feel as though I was failing wholly as a teacher.

How does one *impart* knowledge, allow for the free and easy swinging of a door without hinges? The kids knew the names of authors, and which character asked, in *Julius Caesar,* "Knew you not Pompey?" They had the game-show facts, but the larger arrow missed its mark.

One day a student asked, "Why do we read these books, to understand that we cannot change anything?" The room fell silent. All awaited an answer.

"It is up to the individual to do what he or she can to make the world better. That's why I teach. Maybe I'll show you all that you have the power to do something, if you want to."

Another student raised his voice, "Then why are you leaving us? Why are you going to graduate school?" I didn't have an answer.

I realized after I began teaching that certain inhibitors of the educational process were derived from a social context more dynamic and encompassing an area far greater than my classroom. First, my students saw nothing unusual about grouping themselves on the basis of race and class. It was apparent such divisions presented themselves long before the tenth grade and manifested, to scale, in my classroom. Second, the tenth-grade state writing test was essentially a gauge of skills students had developed over the course of their education. Some of my students could not even read. How were they passed to the tenth grade, or to the ninth, or fifth? In half a semester I couldn't teach a child to read, much less write. Yet that is what I was expected to do, and was judged by way of the test score on the merit of such a child's performance.

These are two problems a teacher faces daily. All I could do was play my part, small though it was. I stopped looking at the big picture and focused on the details of my job, on just the things I was paid to do. But it didn't last long. The kids wouldn't allow it. They asked for the old Mr. P., the *wack P.*, and I realized all the time I'd spent worrying over the failures of the system and of society at large, I'd forgotten about the people it was failing: *the kids*.

So in the time we had left I gave the kids everything I had, except those last words. I had wanted to tell them the long story of my father's life to prove to them that one person really could have an impact, really could do some good in the world. But I had no proof of it, nothing behind it but my own word.

I could have told them, shortly, that there was no such thing as an answer. There was no such thing as a measurable impact, and the only truth is in the search itself, not in seeking to impact at all but merely going about the process of seeking and helping others to seek.

I could have told them something. It could have been anything at that moment because it was the right moment and right moments demand words. I could not provide them. I doubted my ability to impact, the duty of the teacher to impact at all, but mostly the relevance of his words, and I missed my chance.

Teaching is noble in that in exchange for a small extrinsic gain and much aggravation one becomes dedicated to the cause of others, notably children, in a number of capacities. But I wanted more. When I left it I thought, Teaching matters, but I won't base a decision on it. Then I thought, It matters, but I won't base a life on it. My decision was to settle the question of contrary motivations: Does one do well for humanity or for oneself? Which is rule, and which is dictum?

There was more to the choice than that simple problem, for I envisioned in the furtherance of my education the opportunity to address the ills against which a teacher is powerless. Degrees, I thought, are powerful tools, with which one gains the capacity to burrow under the foundations of a system. No system of education can stand apart from the corresponding sociopolitical climate, and when well-meaning lawmakers inflict their policies upon schools, even the simplest processes become fraught with complex problems. An easy solution, I surmised, would be not to introduce new legislation, new tests, and a phantom "accountability." Rather we should free public schools from the bonds of existing rules and invest in teacher training and in teachers, period. Perhaps I would, degree in hand, be one to address these issues, would be the one to effect a positive change for teachers and students in public schools.

I would consign the power of knowledge to the hands of teachers and kids who believe they are its subjects, that they might know the thing is theirs, the world that is, because it is their world, and mine, and yours. I would seek to reinvest some of the power that those in the schools feel they have lost to the vagaries of political debate in the schools themselves, that they might be free to erect a regime that is conducive to learning, not conducive to a bland notion of uniformity enforced by "accountability."

Leaving didn't have to be a selfish choice. Perhaps I could do as much good in the world outside of the classroom and make a better life for myself in the meantime than I ever would have effected as a teacher. I should have told the kids about that, about how one must compromise even on principle. Perhaps I didn't believe myself.

I'm sure I missed an opportunity to clarify, empower, encourage. On the last day I mostly grinned and nodded my head, told the kids to have good summers, be safe, study hard, and find good fortune. They asked me again, "Teach, why are you leaving us?" But I couldn't explain.

My daddy's been bothering me because he knows those kids expected something special. I was afraid to say that I was too unsure about life to render any encompassing wisdom about it. Still, I thought this morning I could have written them a letter, something they could keep and remember me by. It would be a sort of mission statement for the kids with a nice ending. It would read

Dear Student,

I hope I have uncovered just an inkling of what true knowledge is all about: a desire to learn and a willingness to assist the many who need you. Remember, *your* knowledge, *your* wisdom, *your* opinion is *our* future. Together *we* can change things for the better.

Remember, it is the individual who determines the course of the world at large.

Each of you has a special purpose that only you can unveil. Your growth is something profound, the metamorphosis of wishes and dreams into plans, and of plans into action.

There are no small plans, only plans to change the world!

Make this the beginning of your new life, not where you *can* make a difference, but where you *will* make a difference.

Don't ever forget the things we learned together, and don't stop singing.

Sincerely,
Teach

Why I'm Sorry I Don't Teach English

Carol L. Skolnick

I arrived for my student teaching assignment with severely bitten nails and a briefcase full of insecurity. Here I was at last, where I had always wanted to be. I was on the other side of the desk from where I had sat as a rapt and grateful English student only a few years before. Now what was I supposed to do?

And there they were. The untouchables in their denim jackets . . . the nonreaders. A boy in the front row sneaked a shy smile my way and quickly looked down again at his dirty hands. Another was as big as a mountain, and grinned evilly. Brain damage, I was told. A real discipline problem. He was easily twice my size.

"They can't read at all," my cooperating teacher had told me.

"At *all?*" I had asked, incredulous.

"Well, not really. They can't read a book. You'll have to read *Of Mice and Men* aloud to them."

"You mean, they're in the ninth grade and they *can't read?*"

"Just barely. You'll do a separate lesson plan for them, easier test questions, lots of discussion."

Oh.

This wasn't a special education class. This was a room full of misfits. Well, not full of them—there were only nine students. Some were menacing, some were bored, and some were just unhappy. They had all been lumped together as "nonreaders," and they were all daring me to teach them something.

For some reason, I wasn't afraid of them.

I was scared to death of the other ninth graders. They knew an inept college kid when they saw one. And having observed me

99

with them, my cooperating teacher decided not to let me have her senior class. That was just fine with me.

But the nine ninth graders . . . they were a bogus group, a nuisance, throwaways. I just had to get through the syllabus with them any way I could. The easiest way would be to read a book to them.

Well, I wouldn't. I was there to learn, same as them. So what if I made a few mistakes?

Of Mice and Men was in the syllabus for all ninth graders. It was part of the "outcasts in literature" unit. How appropriate for these kids. They'd hate it, for sure.

We barely got through that first class.

I began with some background information on the book, as I had been taught to do—the author, the main characters, the setting. We discussed Lenny, the central character. He was big, strong, too strong for his own good. He was mentally retarded . . .

"Lenny!" one boy suddenly cried, pointing to the mountainous boy, Tom. "Len-nee, Len-nee," the class chanted while Tom retaliated with playful pokes that became not-so-playful punches. He was smiling, but I ached for him. And I prayed they would stop before somebody got hurt, including me. They stopped.

"Who would like to read first?" I asked. No volunteers, of course, so I went around the room. Rather, I *began* to go around the room, but we didn't get very far. The shy boy was first. Plagued with pimples and sweating profusely, he somehow got through a short paragraph and seemed relieved to finish. The taunts continued, this time including him.

We briefly discussed what we had read so far. I read it over to clarify it for myself as well as for them. The boy's reading was truly execrable.

The next reader, a girl, wasn't as bad as the first reader, but she came close. I later learned that she read some things at home—comic books, an occasional teen magazine. There was hope for her, I thought.

Mike, the class clown, was next. "I ain't readin' this," he announced, but it was fairly obvious that he could, as he breezed through a paragraph, mumbled a few sentences, and declared the story to be "bull."

And so it went until the bell mercifully rang. And so it went for the next few days.

Finally, they finished chapter one. And I was in deep trouble.

"Read the book to them, Carol," I was told. "They *must* be tested on this along with the other students. There's a whole list of reading we have to do by next month."

The other classes finished the book and began reading "The Lottery." In my untouchables class, we read about Lenny accidentally killing his puppy.

"Ewww!" "Splat!" "Duhhh, I was only pettin'it, George." "Tom, don't pet me! Please!"

There were a lot of yuks that day. But they got it. And best of all, they were attempting to read.

The other students completed projects at home while they prepared for the exam on the novel. I received some nice dioramas, a comic strip, and several skits. One was a courtroom scene that the students acted out, in which Lenny was cleared of all guilt in connection with Curly's wife's death. They had all read and understood the book, had worked hard, and I gave out many good grades. Most of these students did well on the exam.

But none of their projects and efforts left me as satisfied or touched as I felt the day that Tom, after much hemming, hawing, squirming, and giggling, correctly answered a question in class, without having read so much of a word on his own, because he couldn't.

It has been nearly six years since my student teaching experience. I failed, dismally, on my evaluation. I did not discipline effectively, nor did I engage the attention of my students consistently. I appeared nervous in front of the class. I allowed certain students to dominate class discussions. I was adequately prepared but often became flustered at students' questions and demands, giving them nonanswers when I didn't know what to say. And that class never did finish *Of Mice and Men*.

It took me two more years—one in graduate school, and one spent looking for a job, getting one, and getting fired from it after a month—to realize that teaching was not for me, and I was not for teaching.

Like most student teachers, I had my students fill out report cards for me, to sum up our time together and to tell me what they liked and didn't like. The responses were anonymous, so many were painfully honest. "Could do better if tried harder," one humorist wrote. "Tests were *too hard*," was a common complaint. For every "I loved you," there was a "Sometimes I felt like you hated me."

And then there was the report from one of my nonreaders, nonwriters, nonthinkers, a hopeless case indeed.

"She nice, but don't walk on her. She a good teacher."

Essayist, humorist, and sometime poet CAROL L. SKOLNICK's *writings have appeared in magazines and newspapers (Glamour, The Sun, DM News, The English Journal, AKC Gazette, I Love Cats), in anthologies (Chocolate for a Woman's Dreams, 2001, Simon & Schuster), and on the Web (Salon.com, Paraview, Writer Online, MillenniumSHIFT, and elsewhere). As Web mistress of her own domain, www.EclecticSpirituality.com, Carol explores various spiritual scenes, practices, teachers, and perspectives with a sharp eye and edgy humor.*

To Be or Not to Be a Teacher

Jane Goldenberg

After three years slogging through coursework—child develop-ment, methods, and the increasingly stringent and ballooning bu-reaucratic rules governing teachers—before tackling ten weeks of actual fieldwork in schools on my way to a master's degree in education, one question reverberates through the long, crowded hallways of my cerebrum.

Can I hack it? And I don't mean that I'm wondering if I, a mature career-switcher or career-adder (journalist plus teacher equals . . . workaholic?), can do the job. I'm wondering if anybody will care about all the reading and thinking I've done about the teaching of literature, not to mention my years of professional writing experience. From what I've seen, institutional pressure, time constraints and myriad other nonstudent-centered concerns can quite efficiently round out any youthful square pegs (idealistic naïveté, aka hope) to fit the prevailing professional ethos and/or the ever proliferating standardized tests.

First, let me review some of what attracted me to teaching in the first place. I wanted:

- my avocation to blend with my vocation; I wanted to spend all my time learning, studying universal truths or quests, not ephemera of the business or political world, where new faces and slightly altered situations don't change anything.
- to think about the why, not the what (what newspaper re-porting mostly provides).
- to share what I've already learned about the world, which in-cludes navigating my way through school, with young, eager students, who in my mind are anxiously awaiting my arrival to rescue their otherwise dry and sterile school lives.

- to devote my life to working for the social good, the high-falutin one Plato talks about, not just making money for some commercial purpose (as if).
- to find a way to make a living that could feed my own writing, provide material for better, deeper, more creative thinking. Rereading and rethinking the great works of American and world literature, conferring with my similarly inclined colleagues, and engaging in heated interchanges with my dedicated students would continually stimulate, even electrify, my intellect.

Was this too much to hope for? I think yes. Even though I'm over forty and should know better, I'll admit to being just as idealistic and naive as the next twenty three-year-old hoping to change the world through the great educational system that pretends to open the gateway to upward mobility and a real chance at the American dream, the one poor Jay Gatsby thought he attained. (Already my rereading has come in handy.) Remember him? He's the F. Scott Fitzgerald creation who ended up murdered by the poor cuckolded car jockey suffering from the lethal combo of a muddled brain and the bad influence of a bogus friend with ulterior motives. Is there a parallel here? Am I suffering a bad hangover from drinking too heartily from the cup of high expectations in a world whose answer to high hope is a black eye? Can I be me and a teacher? Or will I turn into something I don't like?

Teachers, who function out of eye- and earshot from each other and most other adults in authority, spend years developing little fiefdoms of pedagogical idiosyncrasies. The prevailing attitudes fall into a few main categories: my method is better than his or hers; method-envy; or what's a method have to do with it? Sure, there are exceptions, teachers who truly embody the hopes I have for myself, but even these teachers faced with classroom realities— kids who don't care, tell you they don't care, regularly cut or readily accept 0's on assignments rather than do them—have adopted methods they surely hated as students and, no doubt, foreswore as novice teachers. Others seem to drift along without community or administrative support, waiting for the day they can finally retire to seemingly greener pastures: another career, the country, administration, anything but this. How to keep your focus on the students' needs and create a student-centered classroom becomes unduly challenging without the cooperation of students, not to mention the enablers in their homes and our media-crazed, short-term, quick-fix society. Each student has an individual agenda as complicated as the school board's.

Many students don't like the teacher before they even walk into the classroom. They think much of what teachers, school, and all adults in authority make them do is wholly irrelevant, especially when they can hope, however futilely, to make a million bucks getting famous surviving the rigors of starvation on some desert island or wherever on national TV. Hey, I'm not so far from being in high school that I don't empathize.

I also hated memorizing a lot of stuff I thought I'd never need again. What exactly do we get from a whole lot of rote memorization for quote retrieval tests anyway? Impressive performances at cocktail parties, job interviews, and other occupations of the adult world, yes. Plus you get good at jumping through hoops, one of the prerequisites for getting along in life. But do these methods teach you how to think more carefully, analytically, creatively? Probably not.

Face it, tests in school don't test merely for knowledge or thinking ability; they test students' diligence, which isn't necessarily a bad goal for school, since to paraphrase one particularly introspective, self-deprecating comedian, 99 percent of life is just showing up. Fact is, many of us have great difficulty with this bare essential. Can't get the job if you don't make it to the interview. But then it's not really English literature or American history (or pick your subject) we're teaching within this educational system. It's learning the ropes of gamesmanship. You play by my rules, and I'll reward you with all the goodies.

If this condition is incontrovertible, and that's a big if, what good can we do-gooders hope to perform in schools? Teach those with the lowest aptitude enough so that they'll know they'll never reach the top rungs of anything? Thank God, the field of education's got a theory to combat that ideal-killer: Howard Gardner's Theory of Multiple Intelligences, which essentially says that while not all people may be destined to be particle physicists, we all have different ways of learning and intelligences that should allow each of us to contribute something and achieve success in some segment of society, whether it be music, carpentry, politics, mathematics, or the humanities (leaving aside how society judges these). Let's emphasize each individual's strengths by offering different pathways to learning.

The problem is that the business of school is mainly an enterprise of words. We take tests by writing, our teachers judge classroom understanding by how well we talk, and, as if I had to state the obvious, those high-stakes tests judge student understanding by how well they read. Teachers become teachers because they're good at writing, talking, and reading. Hardly any students will become teachers. Many won't even make it through school.

Still, I know that if I want to fit in, I'll have to stop identifying with the students. During my observation as I sat in many classrooms, quietly observing the work of veteran teachers, taking my "field notes," I tried to imagine myself up at the head of the class. Instead, what typically happened was that I started to critique the teacher as if I were but another student (or maybe a journalist) in the class. Sometimes, I got really bored.

Imagine what those real students felt. Was it a sign of not yet sufficiently completing my rite of passage across the DMZ, metaphorically speaking we hope, that separates teacher from students? What would it take for me to finish that voyage across, and what would I lose if I did? Would I turn into one of these tired people who give too many quizzes and begin too few discussions or could I be like some of the others I'd seen and talk with my students about books and ideas, thereby expanding the horizons of us all?

Easier said than done.

Getting up in front of five classes a day—which I did during my student teaching—hardly comes under the banner headline: New

Teacher Changes the World, Brings Peace and Understanding Across the Generations and Instills New Desire for Learning. No such miracle occurred while I stumbled my way through my overly ambitious unit plans on *The Odyssey*, *The Great Gatsby*, and Film Narrative/Hitchcock. Just keeping up with all the paperwork regarding attendance, cuts, and behavior reports—not to mention the handouts and planning calendars—taxed my organizational skills.

Then there was the homework I assigned. The students may have thought it was challenging, but the work I created for myself killed any free moment I might have contemplated scheduling. My mentor teacher warned me, but I thought a little challenge would be good for the kids. It took about a week before I understood that he meant the work I was creating for myself, not the students. That was an ah-ha moment that came too late. So I did what any self-respecting teacher does, I muddled through my plan, adjusting it where necessary, killed off some activities, and tried to heed the students' moods by which to inspire them to tackle my assignments.

I may not have seen the perfectly behaved group of students, sparked by the works we were reading into wild and heated discussions about the meaning of life. But I did have the pleasure of seeing some students really connect to what we were doing. I may never really know what kind of impact I had on them. But they taught me that people create better learning experiences than words or books alone so I (and we) better listen to what students say.

Back to the original list. What did I find?

- Teachers spend all their time writing lesson plans (or not), copying worksheets, assignment sheets, explaining and re-explaining them, and grading papers. More attention goes to getting the kids to do their work than reading and rereading the great works.
- As for those universal truths, outside of planning how to spend five productive periods a day with 125–150 students, teachers don't have time to ponder such luxuries.

- Students don't want to hear what teachers have to say about the world. Teachers are the mean test givers, the keepers of the key to graduation and their colleges of choice.
- Schools—at least ostensibly—aren't devoted to the social good. They're devoted to passing increasing numbers of kids through their halls in a timely fashion, pushing and poking them into becoming good standardized test takers.
- There's no time for collegial conversations, and students only regurgitate what you indirectly feed them or what they think you want to hear. By the time they're in high school, they've been practicing this for nine years already, for goodness' sake. Besides, how many students actually really want to read the books if seeing the movie and glancing through the Cliffs' Notes—not to mention the Internet—will get them just as far? Argh.
- Thinking and rereading has to get done on the teachers' own time, which they don't have, and summer gets taken up by summer school, planning for the following year, or taking a trip to the Himalayas—and who can read at such high altitudes?

To be or not to be a teacher. . . . No, I'm not heading into some suicidal daydream. I'm going to the classroom.

Jane Goldenberg *has written articles for numerous publications and is currently working on a novel. She holds two master's degrees from Northwestern University. After earning her master's from the School of Education and Social Policy in 2001, she began teaching seventh-grade language arts at a middle school in Winnetka, Illinois. She is married and has two young children.*

The Template in My Head

Marcia Worth-Baker

Each week of student teaching ended at 2:16 sharp, when the dismissal bell clanged. I think I finally exhaled each of those Fridays around 7:00, when I met a dozen fellow student teachers from my Columbia University program for pizza and beer at V & T's. When a waiter lacked a pen, each of us brandished one. To evenly divide our costs was simple; we all carried scrap paper, pencils, even solar calculators that failed us in the dim restaurant. We were as prepared as we could make ourselves with the tools of our chosen trade and full of sympathy for one another's challenges. It helped us to vent, to grouse a little about missing supplies, looming deadlines, the so far fruitless job hunts. And we shared tips, too, on navigating the New York City Board of Education licensing maze or just finding a bargain on Mr. Sketch markers.

One evening's topic was lesson plans, those all-consuming blueprints for the educational edifices we hoped to build. Many of us found ourselves drowning in paper and ink, squeezing brainstorms into little lined spaces of plan books, or wringing creativity from dry curriculum manuals. Those of us teaching six or seven classes faced six or seven nightly struggles to reduce the whole of American literature, say, to forty meaningful minutes. Then we translated our good intentions into the language of the board of education, including the entry activity known as a "Do Now" and TLW statements. Many of us turned to software, hoping for help. Many programs, then new, promised to cross-reference curriculum standards, make our lessons interdisciplinary, and keep us organized. I certainly needed the help, but I wondered aloud with my classmates if the software-generated lessons would teach the kids in front of us. And would the lessons be interesting for us or for the students?

A veteran teacher, Monica, who joined us that night, listened thoughtfully. "How," one of the student teachers finally asked her, "do you do it? How do you plan all those lessons, all good ideas, all the time? What program do you use?"

Monica laughed. "No software," she said. "But what happens to teachers is this: you develop a lesson plan template in your head. Everything you see or read or experience filters through it. Some things you use immediately; others you save for another year. I don't know if it's good news or bad, but there's so much more to teaching than those curriculum guides."

The conversations soon turned to other matters, to the end of the school year and final projects. On Sunday night, though, I recalled what Monica said as I wrote lesson plans for the coming week. For the kids in the advanced class who were becoming restless, I thought to myself, I might use the brightly colored balls I found on sale in Chinatown earlier that day. I began to scribble in the margins of my plan book. "If your hand lands on the green side, give a detail about a character. Red means a significant plot point. Blue signals an example of a literary technique used in the book." I spoke aloud as I wrote, excited, as my planned review for *Of Mice and Men* took on life as a game, based on something I had seen beyond the schoolhouse walls.

The next day, as I walked through the city's garment district to school, I noticed again the number of machine shops and parts warehouses that lined the streets. They always reminded me of Benji, a student who hadn't found much success or much to interest him in my lessons. Though he was an able reader, Benji was simply bored by fiction, bored by my all-talk, all-writing, no-action style of teaching. He drowsed through school, waking only when a tool, a toy, or a small appliance fell into his hands. Benji liked to tinker and had repaired every pencil sharpener in the school.

"So why not?" I asked the city streets. I stopped at several parts warehouses and asked for catalogs. Without questions, four managers handed me catalogs of machine parts, each equal in size to the Manhattan phone book. Several thousand pages heavier, I staggered to school.

"These are for you," I told Benji bluntly. "Can you figure out the best things in there and report on them to the class? Do it instead of today's lesson."

His eyes widened in surprise.

"What kind of things do you need? What's your project? Your budget? Your specs?" he demanded. "What kind of time do you have?"

"That's up to you, Benji," I said airily. "Tell me what you'd get if you could get anything."

"I'll think about it," he promised, showing more interest than I'd ever seen before. I turned away from him and whispered, "Yes!" to myself. Maybe this idea, coming straight from the template in my head, would work.

Now, ten years later, "Review Ball" is a favorite test preparation strategy for my students. Their summer reading assignment, in fact, is to develop games of "Plot Ball," "Character Ball," and "Setting Ball" based on the books they read. My classroom use of catalogs has mushroomed into a popular extra-credit assignment in which students imagine and describe the restaurants they will run and the stores they will own. And, as Monica predicted, almost everything I see, read, or experience becomes part of my teaching life. Jell-O molds in the shape of the United States turn up at the church rummage sale; next year's fifth graders, who study American history, will have a Jell-O party. The local community school offers fencing, a sport I've always admired; my sixth grade will act out Romeo and Juliet's duel scenes with plastic swords and foils. Scores of ideas haven't survived, of course. The Imagine-You-Lived-in-the-Year-1900 game was a disaster for my twenty-first-century students, though I was deep into turn-of-the-century literature myself. (They didn't want to live in 1900, even in their imaginations, and who can really blame them?) When I returned from jury duty, eager to put the Greek gods we were studying on trial, I reckoned without that troublesome prosecutor, Pandora. All Hades broke loose when she listed Zeus' mortal-world crimes, such as cutting in line and reading others' e-mail. I thank my students for trying, though, and have learned to preface many, many activities with, "Hey, how about we give this a try? I saw/read/found something that I think we'll really like."

I realize now that good teachers do this: they edit the world's vast offerings to meet the curricular (and other!) needs and interests of their students. I didn't know it then, though, as I student-taught. And I certainly had no idea that this ability was already mine, and that it came factory-installed and ready-to-use. When Monica let me in on the secret of the template we teachers carry in our heads, she gave me permission to think harder and more creatively. The success of doing so pushed me further, choosing activities and materials more specifically for the individuals who comprise my classes. Though much has changed, and will continue to alter in the theory and practice of education, the most useful tool I have remains the template in my head, permanent and irreplaceable.

MARCIA WORTH-BAKER *is a graduate of Mount Holyoke College and Columbia University Teachers College. She is the 2001 recipient of the International Reading Association Regie Routman Award and a recipient of Mount Holyoke's Naomi Kitay Award for writing and the New Jersey Association for Gifted Children Grant. Currently, she teaches fourth-, fifth-, and sixth-grade language arts in North Caldwell, New Jersey. She lives in South Orange, New Jersey, with her husband, David, and two children.*

Michael, the Student Who Pushed Me on as a Teacher of Reading

Alis Headlam

In 1970 I started my Master of Education program in Special Education at Lesley College. When I arrived in Cambridge from western Massachusetts, I began looking for a part-time job to support me, and an internship to satisfy the program requirements. I had just completed a series of trainings involving woodworking, automobile mechanics, and small engine repair. Word got around about my vocational interests and I received a call from the director of the Lesley School for Children Pre-Vocational Program asking me if I would be interested in completing my internship there for a small stipend. Even though all of my previous experience was with younger children, I quickly accepted and was assigned to work individually with several students and run a job preparation program.

The pre-vocational program was designed to take children from inner-city schools who characteristically did not fit into the structures of public school. While the kids that came there were labeled as being behaviorally disturbed, I quickly learned that most of them had experienced school failure and had low self-esteem, and this resulted in poor school performance and a lot of acting-out behavior. The pre-vocational program provided them with high-interest activities where academics were stressed through practical application. Classes used few textbooks, so most materials were prepared by the teachers around the vocational subject that was being taught. Students spent a large amount of time each day in a shop atmosphere where they were involved in hands-on activities.

Since classes were small, teachers quickly knew their students well and built a close relationship with them. Maintaining a safe learning environment was of paramount importance, and part of the teacher's role was to spend time daily processing what was happening to the kids in their supervision. I quickly became involved in all aspects of the process as I took kids out for individualized instruction and ran my own class on job preparation.

My story is about how I learned patience and how I learned to overcome disappointment. My story is about Michael, a sixteen-year-old boy from the projects in Cambridge, Massachusetts. He was the oldest of three children and lived with his mother, who was an active alcoholic. Michael, a tall, lanky, sixteen-year-old was the one responsible for caring for the younger children. He was assigned as one of my individual cases because of the anger he displayed in the classroom and because I was already working with him successfully in the job preparation program. In his classroom he was constantly acting out by insulting his female teacher with sexually explicit and sometimes racially explosive comments. She was White and he was Black. After trying to use time-out and suspension, the director of the program decided that he needed some one-on-one tutorial assistance in math and reading. I had arranged for Michael to work in a preschool doing maintenance and he was doing well. His behavior in my job preparation class reflected his sense of accomplishment. We were building a good relationship, I thought.

The first day that Michael came to me in my third-floor attic room, he walked in with a distrustful saunter that said, "You can't make me do anything." And he proceeded to show me that it was true. When I showed him the books that we would be using, he went to the open window and threw them out, turned to me with a look that said, "That's that." Not to be undone, and fearful that I fail my first difficult encounter, I pulled out some dominoes that I was using with another student in math. I began building a tower. Michael observed this from a distance for quite a while before he repeated that I couldn't get him to do anything. I told him, "Well, we have to stay here until the end of the hour so we might as well

114

do something. You can help me build this tower if you want." And he did. For nearly three months Michael came to me every day for an hour and we built towers of dominoes and played checkers, and I taught him to play backgammon. And we talked. All through this time my heart was twisted with doubt about my abilities to teach children whose behavior was troublesome. On Sundays I would sit and write in my journal. Often these sessions ended in tears as I contemplated my failure. The more attached I got to Michael the more painful the week ahead seemed, until one day the school psychologist came to a meeting about Michael. I told him what I was doing and he encouraged me. He told me that no matter how long it took, I needed to build trust with Michael. He gave me the courage to continue.

It happened in January when I least expected it. Michael came to our session and looked at the backgammon board I had set up and said, "OK. Now you can teach me to read." The joy that I felt at that moment cannot be expressed in words. I thought, "We're finally going to do it." And I was confident in my ability to help him. But it was not to be. In the expert judgment of my director, I was no longer needed for the one-on-one instruction. Instead I was assigned full time to a classroom with ten thirteen- and forteen-year-old boys. Even though I pleaded with the director of the program to let me keep one hour daily with Michael, he refused.

Michael's behavior at school went from bad to worse, except in my job preparation class. We maintained a positive relationship, but when I offered to teach him after school he said, "No. They're supposed to teach me during school." For six months, until Michael left school, we remained close. I began a food service program so that students like Michael could work preparing breakfast and lunch for the other students in return for meals and a small stipend. I suspected that Michael began stealing from our cash box. His anger was becoming more and more apparent in every aspect of his relationships at school. The money that was stolen was really a small amount, but the significance of it was not lost on me. I talked to him about it several times, but I could not (and probably did not want to) catch him in the act. Finally, the school was broken into just before graduation and just after a large fundraiser had been completed. Although no incriminating evidence was ever collected, the chief suspect was Michael. Everyone knew how angry he had become and what evidence there was pointed to someone who was angry rather than someone who was stealing for the money. Checks were taken and cash was left behind. Jewelry was strewn about the office of the director and papers scattered around the room.

The last time I saw Michael was about a year after he left our program. He was riding a bicycle down Massachusetts Avenue. Music blared from his headphones as he rode toward me, and he stopped to talk. He told me that he was "going up" for armed robbery the next week. That may have been the last time that I saw Michael in person, but I see and hear him regularly in my mind as I move forward in my career. The vision of his face and the echo of his voice are reminders that make me more determined than ever that no child should ever be denied the opportunity to learn to read. I have dedicated my teaching career to helping other children like Michael, in the hope that in his name one child might be saved.

ALIS HEADLAM *is an educational consultant who works with schools and the community to provide meaningful workshops, seminars, and instruction in the areas of literacy education and the development of racial harmony. She has taught in schools both in the United States and the international community, and has served as a classroom teacher at most grade levels. She has just returned from presenting at the second Pan-African Conference on Reading in Abuja, Nigeria.*

The Ed Block

Beverly Carol Lucey

We took The Ed Block when I was training to be a teacher. A semester-long teacher training program. One measly semester, at a time of great tumult in America, the late '60s. Eight weeks of methods classes led us to eight weeks of practical experience in a school. Then, boom: we were certified.

Most of us didn't know anything about the communities that circled our huge university. We thought everyone would be traumatized and feel the same way we did about the assassinations of MLK and RFK. Surely everyone would be against Vietnam, pro–civil rights, against whatever the police were up to in the Democratic Convention held in Chicago. They weren't. The campus cocoon had kept us from knowing the mood of the farming and factory families around us.

We wanted to change the world, so we went into teaching. We wanted to make it better than it was for us. We were so naive.

The public schools I'd gone to were full of spinsters. They were *old*. They had no sense of humor. They assigned us dull topics. Creativity was a suspicious activity.

I would be different. I'd hated high school, but I would go back, just to make it better for the kids like me.

I was a dope.

Instead of easing my way into a classroom, observing a dedicated teacher, gradually trying this or that . . . I was sent to an old mill town whose claim to fading fame was, at that time, being the home of Tampax.

My 'mentor' was a youngish man who told me within minutes that the only reason he was in the classroom was to avoid Vietnam.

He said he hated the kids. He said he hated this jerkwater town. He was happy to see me.

He turned his schedule over to me on the second day, four out of five classes, keeping the one section he liked, and spent the rest of the eight weeks smoking in the boiler room with the custodians. He did not observe me. He did not give me feedback. During the one class he liked, he farmed me out to other teachers, telling them I would "fill in" if they needed to go somewhere or wanted a break. I don't remember ever seeing him teach.

But here is the odd part about that experience, because what I have told you is still not unusual in many schools. I, who had hated school, who had resisted taking that Ed Block for most of my undergraduate years . . . had found my home.

The space that encircled me and the students felt remarkable. They wore clear faces and dear hearts on their sleeves. They did not try to *get* me. We talked. We wrote together. We ate stories and explored why stories mattered.

They were smart and had never been told that before.

They taught me something wonderful: that in the magic of a classroom, great things can happen if we can push past the rules, the roles, and the automatic rudeness that is a part of the hallway scene.

Theories of education abound. Some ideas contradict each other. Faculty and administrations come and go. The kids? They just keep flowing, filling the room every fall with the possibility and intention of starting fresh.

As teachers, we get the chance to start fresh, too. Every fall we can start over. If I had any words to tell new teachers after thirty years in the classroom, it would be this: let us try to avoid getting caught up in our own small universe and remember who else is out there. Let us, as teachers, make new efforts to find ways to support each other, as well as all the others in the system that support us.

BEVERLY CAROL LUCEY *taught high school English for thirty years in Massachusetts. After moving to Georgia, she joined the education faculty at Agnes Scott College and is the Coordinator of Field Experiences, placing and supervising student teachers. Her website for educators is LanguageWrangler.com.*

A Classroom Exchange

Dennis Donoghue

On my last day of student teaching sixth graders, I called one of my students a rotten little bastard. Maybe I did it because I knew I'd never see the kid again, or because he had driven me crazy for eight weeks. I should not have said it—I knew that much—but I couldn't help myself. The words just came out: you rotten little bastard.

It was the spring of 1976. Each morning after breakfast in the university dining hall, I would climb into a Rambler station wagon along with five other student teachers for the ride across town to Memorial Elementary. I carried a box lunch that had been placed on my breakfast tray—roast beef on Wonderbread, Hostess cup-cakes, a Red Delicious apple as hard as a marble. I wore polyester bell-bottoms, a Banlon shirt, and crepe-soled loafers I had bought for seven dollars.

The university did not offer education as a major. Instead we had an education program, which meant you had the option of teaching elementary school during the second semester of junior year as a break from loftier academic goals.

On the first morning of my student teaching, Miss Hanson introduced me to her class, asked me to say a few words about myself, then left to use the bathroom. I told the students I lived in a dorm, ran distance events on the track team, and that I had a girlfriend. "What's her name?" asked Stephanie. Before I could answer, Jimmy said, "Mr. Donoghue, what's an erection?" The class stared at me. A few kids snickered while I fished for something witty or informative to say.

"Is it this?" Jimmy held up his arm, his hand balled into a fist. Slowly he uncurled his index finger until it was straight, then arched it upward.

"Put your arm away," I said.

Jimmy pretended to force his arm into his desk when Miss Hanson returned and asked the class to take out their spelling workbooks. I moved to a table by a window to take notes. Stephanie and Rochelle turned and studied me.

Later, at recess, Jimmy told me that he had a near genius IQ. His right to say whatever he wanted to say, he claimed, was protected by the U.S. government. He told me the sun gave him hives and that was why he was so pale. He was also thin, had a large head and wore eyeglasses similar in style to the pair I wore.

"Let's trade to see who's blinder," he said. "Come on, the other student teachers let me do it."

When I said no he said he was getting contact lenses anyway.

"Why don't you wear contact lenses?" he asked me. "Everyone your age does now. Are you afraid you'll blind yourself?"

"My work study job checking IDs at the university swimming pool doesn't cover the cost of my meal plan," I said, telling him more than I thought he needed to hear.

"Don't you have parents? Can't they pay for them?"

He badgered me with more questions. I told him I didn't want to talk to him, that I wanted to get to know other students. He claimed I didn't like him.

The next week I began my class project, a newspaper I called *Colonial Times*. Jimmy wrote and illustrated an article on horse-racing.

"This belongs on the front page," he said, "above the fold."

"We're leading with something about the Revolution," I said.

"Hey, it's a light news day. Why not this?"

I could see he'd put a lot of work into his piece. The content was entertaining, the cursive script easy to read, the horses drawn with anatomical clarity.

"In sports," I said. "The back page."

"There was no sports section at that time in history."

"No," I said, though I wondered what I would have said had another kid produced this kind of work.

"You hate me."

He tore his paper in half and skulked to his seat, telling his classmates not to submit anything because of the editor's lack of vision. Randy told him to shut up, then asked him for a quarter for lunch or else he'd wring his neck.

"Randy, do your work," I said.

"Send him to the office for threatening another student," Kelly instructed me.

"I wouldn't," Jimmy said to me. "It'll look like you can't control the class. Then you won't get a passing grade. You'll end up teaching in some foreign country as a member of the Peace Corps."

A week later the class finished the first and only edition of the *Colonial Times*. We made copies on the mimeograph machine and distributed them around the school. Jimmy announced he was boycotting the newspaper and encouraged other kids to do the same.

"That rag isn't worth the paper it's written on," he said.

On my last day the students presented me with a polished wooden apple inscribed with my name and the name of the school. Miss Hanson gave me a coffee mug and a thank-you card scented with Shalimar. At 2:15 the kids filed past me, following Miss Hanson to their buses. Jimmy drifted from the end of the line.

"You're the worst student teacher we've ever had," he said, "and since we've had them since the first grade, that's saying something."

"You rotten little bastard," I said.

He gasped, as if I'd thumped him on the chest.

"You can't talk to me like that," he said.

That night Miss Hanson called me at my dorm. Jimmy's parents had spoken to the principal and had also notified Professor Munson, who headed the education program.

"For the record," I told her, "He's lying."

Professor Munson's office was on the bottom floor of the social sciences building. It had no windows and smelled of cigarettes.

"There's nothing to tell," I said when he asked me to describe the incident. "He claims I called him a rotten little bastard."

Professor Munson broke the ash off his Pall Mall into a paper coffee cup and coughed. He glanced at his watch.

"Did you?"

"No," I said.

"Teaching elementary school isn't for everyone," he said. "Kids can be merciless. They know how to hit your sore spot. They can make you say things you'd never say to a colleague, a roommate, or a spouse for that matter."

"He's lying," I said. "He made the whole thing up."

A few minutes later Professor Munson saw me to the door.

"Consider this a lesson," he told me, "one that's not in the textbook."

I received a grade of B for student teaching. The students teachers I traveled with each morning all got A's, which made me think that Miss Hanson and Professor Munson didn't believe me, that I'd been penalized for lying and then denying that I'd lied, though I'd never been told outright and didn't bother to ask. That summer an IBM card arrived in the mail. It stated that I was certified to teach grades K–8 in Massachusetts. I put the card in a cedar box on top of my dresser that held my passport, some silver dollars, a tie clasp my brother had given me for being best man at his wedding, and a roach clip with faux eagle feathers I'd bought at an Indian reservation.

Now, twenty-five years later, the young teachers on my team ask me how I am able to choose my words so carefully in the midst of a confrontation with one of our sixth graders. They want to know what to say and how to say it, afraid that in the heat of the moment they'll utter something they'll regret. They want to know my secret.

I tell them nothing beats experience, then suggest strategies that work for me. I do not tell them I once called a student a rotten little bastard and then denied it. But I do tell them that they should adhere to a standard of conduct, for what seems intolerable one day won't be the next. Once hurtful words are spoken, I warn them, those words cannot be taken back. The words I spoke to Jimmy will stay with me always, and chances are they're still with him too. It seems as if I'd etched them in stone, those four words which slipped so easily from my tongue on that spring day many years ago.

DENNIS DONOGHUE teaches sixth grade in Salisbury, Massachusetts. His work has appeared in several publications including Teacher Magazine *and* Adoption Today. *He and his wife, Carla Panciera, live in Rowley, Massachusetts, with their three daughters.*

Street Syllabus

Tekla Dennison Miller

A male captain greeted me on my first day as the deputy warden of Huron Valley Women's Prison, saying, "What training did you have for becoming a deputy?" A second male captain nodded in agreement.

I knew what they thought—that they were far more qualified than I, they had been in the trenches longer, and that I had not yet paid my dues. So my answer was, "I taught fifth grade in South Central Los Angeles, also known as Watts."

Though the two men glared at me with dumbfounded expressions, I decided not to explain my history to them. I was confident that their egos couldn't handle the fact I was a veteran of combat from the Fifty-ninth Street Elementary School in the sixties just after the Watts riots and my training was far more valid for a prison setting outside Detroit than their entrenchment in rural White America.

There were thirty-seven children in that class. Ten of them could read at the fifth-grade level. The only three Caucasian students were Mexican and could not speak English. I was twenty-four years old, and this was my first teaching job. Well, let me clarify that.

Because of the riots, no one wanted to work in Watts' schools. In order to fill the needed number of teaching positions, the Los Angeles School Board agreed to let second-semester student teachers work full time for five-sixths of the actual teacher's salary. In reality I was graded as a student teacher, having not yet graduated from the University of California, Los Angeles, but was teaching full time as a permanent substitute, for real money. Despite the income, I was still an inexperienced student teacher, and I was scared.

Teaching in Watts meant I was responsible for every subject, whether I knew anything about them or not—physical education, art, music, and all the academics. The first time I took my class of well-seasoned, streetwise fifth graders to the yard for PE, they left. All thirty-seven disappeared by going over, under, and through the fence surrounding the yard. Cemented helplessly in place by panic, I watched them flee and when the last one disappeared into the depths of the neighborhood filled with boarded up buildings and empty lots, I mustered up the courage to make my confession to the principal. She was a large, no-nonsense, African American, middle-aged woman to whom I confided, "I don't have a class."

She squinted at me over glasses that perched on the end of her nose. "Just what do you mean, young lady? What do you mean you have *no* class?"

"They're all gone," I whispered and then explained what had happened, while she tapped a pencil against her desk. I felt like a child caught stealing a Snickers candy bar from the corner store. I desperately wanted to suck my thumb.

She stopped tapping long enough to let me know, "These boys and girls will be little hoodlums if you let them." She shook the pencil in my face. "Don't ever take your eyes off them." She clipped those orders like a Marine drill sergeant.

I learned from the principal that short of corporal punishment, unless administered by her, I was allowed to use any means of control in my classroom. I chose the "Master Blaster." He was the number one soul disc jockey in Los Angeles then and a good friend. One day, he lectured the thirty-seven troublemakers on the importance of hard work and education. He shared his personal experiences, which included working his way through college as a janitor. Now I admit, an outsider would probably have had difficulty understanding how the Master Blaster could influence any child. He wore his short black hair with bangs that formed a peak ending just above his nose, and dressed in a black cape, black pants tucked into black leather knee-high boots, and a black turtleneck sweater. Yet what the King of Soul did in an hour I couldn't have accomplished in a year, evidenced by the wide-eyed devotion on every student's face as the King lectured while dancing up and down the rows of desk swirling his cape. The Master Blaster's appearance that day in my school room won me a position among the top people in the country in the students' estimation—right up there with Martha and the Vandellas, The Temptations, Little Richard, and Smokey Robinson.

Angela, however, was not won over by this scheme. She was a bright, ten-year-old who outweighed everyone in the class and maybe a few students put together. She was also taller than everyone else, even me. I had learned from the principal not to turn away from the class for longer than a few seconds for fear someone would get maimed, including me. I forgot that rule the day Gary, the smallest student, punched Angela in the nose. When I heard the "splat," I averted my attention from the math problem I was writing on the board and was confronted by Angela's bloody nose, and by her screaming, "Gary hit me." She pointed a chubby finger at the assailant as her chocolate-colored face turned to shades of red.

"Go wash your face in the bathroom, Angela," I ordered.

"Aincha goin ta do nothin ta Gary?" She asked, blood trickling across her mouth and down her chin. There were no tears.

"No. You deserved it after all the things you have done to him."

Angela stood up with such force her chair toppled to the floor in a loud crash. The other students, fear showing in their eyes, held their breath as they watched Angela clench and unclench her fists. She narrowed her eyes at me, her lips thinned out as blood vessels pulsed with anger at the edges of her forehead. I waited for her to leap at me. Instead, she turned on her heels and left the room—for the day. I didn't report her absence to the principal.

A smile replaced Gary's usual grumpy, old-man's expression as his eyes followed Angela's exit. When the door slammed behind her, Gary appeared to grow as he wallowed in his first victory over anyone. Up until that time, he hardly spoke, and shrunk each time Angela or another student made fun of him.

"When ya goin to grow, little boy?"

"Where'd ya mother get your clothes, from the garbage?"

"You're nothin but a weenie."

And of course Gary was always picked last for baseball, when a bat and ball could be found.

After class the next day and everyone had left, Angela approached me as I graded papers at my desk. She stood, feet planted wide apart and both hands on her ample hips, looking like a Sumo wrestler. Her firm mouth remained rigid as she warned, "I'm tellin my mother what ya did to me yesterday," she smirked with intimidation. "She's gonna come here an kick yo ass." I was somewhat startled, but cocky when I answered, "Well, Angela, if that is the only way I can get her in here to talk to me, by God, bring her on."

I never met Angela's mother, but Gary, uttering few words, carried my books to and from my car every day after the bloody nose incident. Angela, on the other hand, pulled a switchblade on me a week later. We were alone in the classroom. I had forced her to stay after school to finish an assignment. I guess that completing her school work didn't make her happy.

Clutching the knife, she kept her distance from me. I cowardly remained behind, and protected by, my desk, though I sensed Angela was trying to scare me and was not prepared to use the weapon. I hoped my intuition was right when I challenged her. "You know, you live in a neighborhood where if you pull a knife on someone you better use it and fast before someone uses it on you. Otherwise, you'll end up dead."

Angela held that knife in her hand for several moments never taking her angry eyes off me. Neither of us spoke. Other than my tension-filled breathing the ticking clock was all that could be heard. Then, for reasons I will never understand—fear, hope for a better future, not wanting to be a bully anymore—Angela placed the switchblade on my desk and finished her lesson. I slipped the weapon into the drawer and tried not to convey my unabashed relief. I didn't want Angela to know I had been frightened of her. Since I knew Angela would be expelled, I never told the principal about Angela's threats. My list of secrets kept from the drill sergeant of the Fifty-ninth Street School had grown long.

I'm not going say Angela's behavior changed by leaps and bounds after that. Any positive strides made in that rundown inner-city classroom would most likely have been eroded by her environment. Just as a rock outcropping eventually succumbs to the stronger environmental influence of water flowing over it, so would Angela succumb to her environment. Yet there were subtle differences, especially when I chose her to be the teacher's assistant or when I asked her to tutor one of the Mexican students. And though she saw her worth could be proved without a knife or fists, she didn't stop teasing Gary. He, however, continued to stand up to Angela and they eventually became friends.

Over the years I have thought about all the Angelas and Garys I knew at the Fifty-ninth Street Elementary School. I wonder how many ended in prison or whether they are still alive. I am hopeful that some finished high school.

I finally graduated from UCLA with my teaching certificate in hand. I was certain that what I had learned from my student teaching primed me for any life challenge or adventure. Over the years I have taught off and on, mostly substituting, but made my career in corrections.

Those two captains probably never saw the likes of Angela until they worked in a prison. They never got the benefit of Angela's instruction. She taught me to talk my way through difficult situations rather than fight my way out. Angela, in her way, also trained me to be a humane warden focused on educating, rather than punishing, prisoners.

Yet I often wonder where the Master Blaster is when I need him today.

TEKLA DENNISON MILLER, *author of* The Warden Wore Pink *(Biddle Publishing, 1996), is the former warden of two maximum security prisons and taught in the mid-sixties in Watts, California, after the riots. She is now a criminal justice consultant living and writing in Colorado.*

We Learn from Our Mistakes

Susan C. Voorhees

We learn from our mistakes? . . . Let me say that in a more definite tone . . . we learn from our mistakes. Student teaching is probably one of the best experiences a teacher-in-training will have; student teaching is a learning mechanism. I can say that now with no hesitation because my student teaching experience occurred seventeen years ago, and while I still revisit these experiences in my head, I will never be the "stressed out" novice I was the first day I entered Ms. Ferris' second-grade classroom and was introduced as the new student teacher, "Miss Vellecca."

Here's another saying, "Everything happens for a reason." It took me quite a long time to appreciate that one, particularly after I humiliated myself in front of Ms. Ferris' second-grade class and my student teaching supervisor. I can think of only one thing that a new student teacher has greater angst over than her first day of student teaching, and that is the first day she is *observed* student teaching. Let me revisit the day I decided I would never teach again.

Three days prior to the day my student teaching supervisor would observe me, I conscientiously approached my cooperating teacher and asked for some advice. "My supervisor said she would like to observe a language arts lesson; can you help me?" I meekly asked. My cooperating teacher smiled and responded, "What would you like to teach?" (Teachers will forever answer a question with a question.) If I knew that, I wouldn't be asking for help, I thought, but decided not to verbally articulate. Frantically searching my brain for an intelligent response, I looked over her shoulder and noticed some antonyms and synonyms that Ms. Ferris had listed on the board for her students as independent seat work. My brain now in gear, I thought how easily the class was able to match antonyms and synonyms today. In fact, these children have been doing this for the last week. If I make antonyms and synonyms my topic, I bet most of the class will come up with the correct answers, and I will look as if I taught them well. "What about antonyms and synonyms?" I responded. Ms. Ferris shook her head in agreement. She provided several ways to go about doing this, but I was thinking about how much children love games, so after she had spent several minutes providing old lesson plans and materials, I decided I would create a game involving matching antonyms and synonyms. My lesson went something like this:

First, I would tape a bare apple tree and bare maple tree, made from poster paper, to the blackboard. Second, I would place attachable word cards in the shape of apples and leaves mixed together in one pond on the floor. Each apple card would have one antonym written on it and each leaf card would contain one synonym. Third, I would define antonyms and synonyms with the class and write these definitions on the board. Fourth, I would divide the class into two teams and put them in two different lines, one on each side of the room, like a spelling bee. Fifth, I would explain the rules of the game: I would provide the first student in line with a target word and ask that student to go to the pond and find the antonym or synonym card that matched the target word. No one on the team could help. If the student provided a correct response, then he or she would place the antonym or synonym card on the appropriate tree. If the student was unable to correctly locate the word in ten seconds, then that student would have to sit down. This would follow in a like manner until there was no one left on a team or there were no more words left in the pond; both trees would be filled. Understanding the importance of motivation and rewards, the winning team would have no homework. Very clever and well thought out, don't you think?

The night before my language arts lesson, I diligently worked on my word trees, carefully cutting out each apple and leaf. How beautiful my trees looked. I then memorized a clear definition for each word, antonym and synonym, spent quite a bit of time picking out the perfect skirt and blouse, and went to bed, nervous but confident.

The next morning, Ms. Ferris reminded the students that I was going to be observed, and because she liked me, she threatened them that they had better behave ... or else. What a nice woman, I thought. Soon after that, my supervisor arrived. I escorted her to the back of the room. Providing a few more words of encouragement, Ms. Ferris left me alone with her students (and my supervisor, of course).

The lesson began as planned, defining the words *antonym* and *synonym*. I was sure my supervisor was very impressed. I then restated the definitions I had memorized, divided the class into two teams, and explained the rules. Then the game began. Addressing the first student in line on Team One, I stated, "The word is *large*. Can you find the antonym?" This student quickly walked up to the pond, located the word *small*, placed the apple card on the appropriate tree, and returned to the end of the line. Turning to Team Two, I stated the word *jump* and asked for the synonym. Student number two was also able to locate the correct response. I was very pleased, thinking teaching is really not that difficult. I continued randomly calling out antonyms and synonyms, but before long, the students began to talk to one another while they waited for their turn. I explained that one of the rules was no talking, but even as I restated this, students were not paying attention. Then Joey, a child with special needs, gave an incorrect response, which signaled a teammate to taunt that he would be blamed if the team lost the game. Moreover, a devilish student named Danielle decided she would rather talk and braid her friend's hair. I reprimanded her several times, but by now half the class was fooling around. I can remember thinking, I've got to do something quickly. I glanced over at my supervisor, who gave me a nonverbal gesture of encouragement. But I could sense she was not overwhelmingly pleased with my lesson. And then, as often happens when one is inexperienced, I panicked and said, "The next person who speaks loses the game for the whole team!"

My hope was that my threat would scare my students into behaving and paying attention. And it worked, for a few seconds anyway. But, as the old saying goes, "There is always one in every group." Danielle whispered something to her friend, which caused her teammate to laugh, which in turn, caused a few others to laugh. I turned to Danielle and said sternly, "Did you say something?"

"No," she arrogantly responded. Now this was a dilemma. Do I carry out my threat or do I let it go?

"Danielle, you were talking, and therefore, your team loses." Danielle's team was now shouting at Danielle and Danielle was shouting at me saying that she wasn't talking and it wasn't fair. I then began bickering back and forth with this second grader as she blamed others for talking. At this point, the class was completely out of control. And then, I said something that to this day I can't believe came out of my mouth.

"YOU LIAR," I shouted at Danielle.

Then there was silence.

My supervisor ended my lesson. I was devastated and at that very moment vowed never to teach again, and not even to go back after lunch. But I did. And since I am now a college professor of education (who happens to supervise student teachers), you can see that I didn't quit as I would have liked, but instead "learned from my mistakes."

What did I learn? First, while at the time I thought it was a good idea to teach something that the students could do independently, I now realize that it is not teaching if all the students have already acquired that knowledge; no learning (at least about synonyms and antonyms) took place that day. Children need to see a purpose in what is being taught. Second, good teaching has less to do with gimmicks (like playing games) and more to do with teachers having the knowledge to assess students' needs and interests and base their instruction accordingly. Third, all children need to be involved. Planning instruction that included a response from only one child at a time was not good management and did not encourage ongoing thinking for all. Fourth, threatening students is not an effective classroom management technique; it diminishes teacher-student trust. Finally, students should compete within themselves to improve, not with one another.

Do I still wish that day never happened? Absolutely. At the time did I think I would ever share this nightmare teaching experience with future teachers? Absolutely not. Will other student teachers learn from my mistakes? I'd like to think so.

SUSAN C. VOORHEES is an assistant professor of education at Long Island University/Southampton College, where she teaches both undergraduate and graduate courses in literacy assessment and methods. Her research interests include early literacy development, family literacy, reading motivation, and teacher education. Prior to college teaching, she taught kindergarten and second grade.

Thanks to Kay

Alexa L. Sandmann

Kay Thomas.

In my own personal Educators Hall of Fame, Kay Thomas would be the first inductee. She was my cooperating teacher when I student taught.

She changed my life.

Her office was tiny, sandwiched between the two classrooms in which she taught. It was in that office that she and I met and negotiated what I was going to teach during the quarter. We ended up with Hawthorne's *The Scarlet Letter*. Was she crazy, I thought? I had read *The Scarlet Letter* as a junior in high school myself and found it exceedingly challenging, and I was in an "honors" class. How would these "regular" juniors handle it, I wondered. "They will," she said, "if we support them. And you will," she concluded with a smile. Her enthusiasm was contagious. I found myself drawn to her immediately as she talked animatedly about each of her classes, characterizing her day.

I'd like to say I could hardly wait to begin my student teaching and although I knew this placement had been a gift (I didn't have the hourlong commute most of my classmates had), at that point in my life I had no intention of being a teacher. Teaching was only my "insurance policy." Society had taught me well that valedictorians don't become teachers. In the era of the film *Annie Hall*, from which the saying was popularized, "Those who can't, teach, and those who can't teach, teach gym," education was not considered a profession for the academically talented.

So, I had actually begun my college career as a French major, with dreams of translating at the United Nations. When I decided

French wasn't special enough, that a more exotic language like Japanese would be required, I switched to English. Still, I had enough credits to become a French teacher, so I graduated with dual degrees, a bachelor of arts in English, with a minor in French, as well as a bachelor of science in secondary education.

But not having graduated yet, I began my student teaching experience one bitterly cold January morning. Because in teacher education programs of my generation field placements were rare and included a minimal number of hours, student teaching was really more about classroom management. For Mrs. Thomas, however, teaching was about the students, for they were always at the center of her thinking.

Her lessons for me were numerous, but they started with these core principles:

On respect: If you respect your students, they will respect you.
On rules: Create only as many as necessary—and enforce them.

The hallmark of her educational philosophy was whether the students learned. While she was an expert in addressing the curriculum required by the district, covering it was not her mission, even if she nearly always did. She often re-taught; I thought her incredibly patient as she re-thought and re-focused lessons. I soon came to realize that it was in the "re-teaching" where the learning truly occurred. As a writing teacher now, I realize the re-teaching of the learning process is the revising aspect of the writing process. It's where students and teachers "re-see," or "re-vision" their work together. She adapted, made changes, and shared again, always to her students' gain. I quickly learned from watching her that if something were worthy of study the first time but wasn't learned, why wouldn't I circle back so students were successful the second, or even third time?

She had no discipline problems because she was always right there with the students, both physically and psychologically. She had the "with-it-ness" only master teachers have. No one was bored or frustrated. She moved through the classroom during discussion like a first-string quarterback running through the lines, constantly looking for opportunities to slip timely bits of information or just the right question into the conversation like the quarterback throws the football given just the right opening. I watched in awe. I learned.

On discipline: If classes are interesting, students will be interested.

On creativity: Be as engaging and innovative as possible. "Same old" is boring—for everyone.

On homework: Assign only as absolutely necessary, and students will complete it.

On student lethargy: Talk to the passive student individually, out in the hall, before or after class—never in front of others.

One Monday during morning announcements, only a few weeks after I had begun, I learned there had been an automobile accident. One of the students in my fourth-hour class had died. Several students walked into the classroom, looked at his empty seat, and began to cry. I wasn't sure what to do. I hadn't gotten to know that young man very well yet, just as I didn't know his classmates that well yet. My impulse was to "address the issue," let the students talk, but what I feared was that I was supposed to be teaching. Isn't "just talking" a cop-out? A sloughing off of my teacherly duties? After all, I was a student teacher. I had to prove myself each day.

Kay came to my rescue. She led the discussion as classmates tearfully reminisced, eyes continually drawn to their classmate's empty chair as if they could somehow will him back into their lives. When tissues were spent and heartache was eased as emotions were released, at least temporarily, Kay suggested I continue with *The Scarlet Letter* but allow students to work independently, not discussing issues as a class as I had planned. I did, weaving throughout the classroom and answering questions as they were asked, sometimes just touching a shoulder to let the student know it was okay to remember and cry. The work could be considered tomorrow; the reality of the event overtook the agenda.

On humanity: Adjust lesson plans to fit student emotions.
On flexibility: Be flexible; adjust schedules to accommodate student learning, not school or teacher convenience.

Other lessons would prove useful.

On school politics: They exist. Know people's positions and adjust responses appropriately.
On fights: Don't get between the combatants. Talk to them and send for help.

Kay delighted in her students. She nudged them into thinking more deeply than they had wanted to and was as joyous as they were by the results. She smiled at them, continually. While the rapt attention of her students may have suggested to an outsider that she followed the management adage, "Don't smile until Christmas," I'm sure she smiled at all of her students, even on the first day of school. That smile invited them into her classroom and into her heart—and they knew it.

On humor: Use it, in a playful, nurturing way. No sarcasm.

In the most powerful lesson of all, Kay told me about a conversation she and her uncle had. He was an avid gambler, especially of the "ponies" at the racetrack. She had been trying to explain to him her strategy for a particular student. His response? "You mean you'd work that hard for one student out of thirty? Those odds are 30 to 1. I'd never make that bet." But Kay did, every day.

On diversity: Treat students equally, which does not necessarily mean the same. Give each student what he or she needs.
On expectations: Aim high. Scaffold the information to make success inevitable—if the student is willing to do the work.
On commitment: Work hard, very hard; teaching is a year-round enterprise, with lesson planning an ongoing cognitive activity.

At the end of student teaching that winter quarter, I left Ohio for spring break in Boston where I had several interviews with companies in the retail business. What else does an English major do—if she doesn't teach? I loved Boston but not retail and realized that what I had discovered about teaching while student teaching was my truth now.

I loved teaching.

While every job application I had completed before student teaching had been for an entry-level position in a bank or a store, every application I returned afterward was for a teaching position in a school district.

Kay's lessons for me were ones that would need reinforcement and refinement as I more fully discovered my own teaching style, especially after a less-than-satisfying beginning to my first year of teaching, but when I found the next teaching position and lived it for the year, I knew I had found what I was called to be—a teacher. Not just a teacher, but *a teacher*—a curricular leader, academic role model, nurturer of learners, supporter of individuals.

Now I teach at a university, in a college of education. Recently a former student of mine, who had just finished student teaching, beamed as she came to my children's literature class one evening.

"I'm substituting," she told me, nearly glowing with excitement. "I can't believe I'm getting paid to do what I love."

I know. Thanks to Kay and her willingness to invite an apprentice into her classroom and generously spend the considerable time it takes to mentor well, I came to truly understand the work and, more important, the wonder of teaching. For it is the wonder that has kept me in the classroom for twenty-five years now.

I can imagine myself in no other place, thanks to Kay.

In her tenth year in education at the University of Toledo, DR. ALEXA L. SANDMANN specializes in children's literature and writing; she directs the Toledo Area Writing Project. She has published in various national journals. Her book, with colleague Jack Ahern, Linking Literature with Life: The NCSS Standards and Children's Literature for the Middle Grades, *is scheduled for publication in 2002.*

Duty Free

Davi Walders

Rain splashes the windows as the ferry rocks. We, who have ridden hours trying to see her, peer again through steamed windows and darkness, but the mighty woman with a torch has taken cover for the night. Lady Liberty hides, backlit in heavy mist, leaving us only a blur of wet luminescence.

We have waited years for this: the simple pleasure of riding a whole dripping day out—down Seventh Avenue, the ferry to Staten Island and back, the bus up Sixth to the Park, then back down again—together. Two friends, one who has flown across continents and oceans; the other who has driven highways and freeways north. We have come far to reconnect. The steady downpour wipes away separation and distractions, syncopates speech, memory, and laughter.

Years ago we worked together. Then we were teachers, serious, learned. Our high heels and our dresses made us serious. We were learned to the extent that we had learned a language or two earlier than the students we were teaching, on whom we had at least a decade.

In those days, we had to wait fifty minutes to reconnect, to let the bell mark the end of class five times a day, unleashing adolescents glum from verb conjugation and grammar exercises to plow through the door in search of the day's romantic interest. And leaving us to each other and hall duty.

We were young and lucky. Lucky to find each other in the same school, classrooms across the hall. Lucky to be stuck every year with hall and bus duty. Standing outside between classes, monitoring drab green-tiled halls, ever slamming lockers, slick-as-an-ice-rink floors, and at day's end, lucky to be in charge of checking the endless line of yellow buses until the last pulled out. We were lucky to have each other during the dirty work of being teachers. Principals roamed the halls, monitoring our monitoring, inspecting suspicious things, whispering into walkie-talkies. But we kept our cover.

We had our real business of talking and laughing. We needed no walkie-talkies. We stayed connected through hall duty sound bites, five minutes on the hour. Like convicts allowed short visits, we laughed and cried and mastered life sharing while being evaluated on how dutifully we hall-, bathroom-, and bus-dutied. We had been given our charge—to stop students from running, chewing, shoving, kissing, killing, hugging, fighting. We did our duties, looked serious, and kept talking.

The years of early adulthood, paying our dues, doing what we had to do. On hall duty, we raised children, straightened out marriages, made decisions, shared fantasies and dreams. In between the precious five-minute breaks, there were the thousands of hours in square cinderblock rooms—French, room 102; Spanish, room 103. Five classes a day, 150 exams a night. Hard work, but we had hall-, bathroom-, and bus-duty time, each other, and laughter.

Two women in the hall, wiping chalk dust off our hands, trying to get purple mimeograph ink off our skirts, teaching and talking. But mainly, in five-minute slices we carved ourselves out, still sorting the issues of the day out in the parking lot at dusk, packing ourselves and kids into a Corvair for spring break, spreading picnics in the summer, trying to grow ourselves and our own children up.

Now there is only the rain, the rocking, and the ferry motor. Slamming lockers and hall huggers are gone; our children are grown. We are beyond lives lived in breaks and sound bites. Today, we have the luxury of twenty-four slow, slippery hours.

I tell you this now. Make early for yourself a friend who will chew the bones of life with you. Find that one person who will do hall duty, bus duty, child duty, marriage duty, parent duty, work duty. Wipe the dust off your hands together. Expect lives lived on separate continents. Build a fence around memory and laughter.

And wait. A time will come—on a bus, train, or a deck in the rain, for riding the whole day out past a shrouded woman in the fog who stands guard over two women lost in unbroken conversation and laughter.

DAVI WALDERS is a writer and education consultant whose poetry and prose have appeared in more than 150 publications. Her awards include an Alden B. Dow Creativity Fellowship and a 2001 Maryland State Arts Council Grant in Poetry. She founded and directs the Vital Signs Poetry Project at the National Institutes of Health and its Children's Inn in Bethesda, Maryland.